DEMOSTHENES, SPEECHES 60 AND 61,
PROLOGUES, LETTERS

THE ORATORY OF CLASSICAL GREECE

Translated with Notes • *Michael Gagarin, Series Editor*

VOLUME 10

DEMOSTHENES, SPEECHES 60 AND 61, PROLOGUES, LETTERS

Translated with introduction and notes by

Ian Worthington

 UNIVERSITY OF TEXAS PRESS, AUSTIN

First edition, 2006

Requests for permission to reproduce material from this work should be
sent to Permissions, University of Texas Press, P.O. Box 7819, Austin, TX
78713-7819. www.utexas.edu/utpress/about/bpermission.html

⊚ The paper used in this book meets the minimum requirements of
ANSI/NISO Z39.48-1992 (R1997) (Permanence of Paper).

Library of Congress Cataloging-in-Publication Data
Demosthenes.
    [Selections. English. 2006]
    Speeches 60 and 61, Prologues, Letters / Demosthenes ; translated with
introduction and notes by Ian Worthington. — 1st ed.
        p.   cm. — (The oratory of classical Greece)
    Includes bibliographical references and index.
    ISBN-13: 978-0-292-71331-4 (cloth : alk. paper)
    ISBN-10: 0-292-71331-2 (cloth : alk. paper)
    ISBN-13: 978-0-292-71332-1 (pbk. : alk. paper)
    ISBN-10: 0-292-71332-0 (pbk. : alk. paper)
    1. Demosthenes—Translations into English.   2. Speeches, addresses,
etc., Greek—Translations into English.   3. Athens (Greece)—Politics and
government—Early works to 1800.   I. Worthington, Ian.   II. Title.
III. Series.
PA3951.E5   2006
885'.01—dc22

                                                            2006011488

For
Marianne McDonald
philomousos, scholar, philanthropist, friend

CONTENTS

〰〰〰〰〰〰〰〰〰〰〰〰〰〰〰〰〰〰〰〰〰〰〰〰〰〰〰〰〰〰〰〰〰〰〰

SERIES EDITOR'S PREFACE

This is the tenth volume in a series of translations of *The Oratory of Classical Greece*. The aim of the series is to make available primarily for those who do not read Greek up-to-date, accurate, and readable translations with introductions and explanatory notes of all the surviving works and major fragments of the Attic orators of the classical period (ca. 420–320 BC): Aeschines, Andocides, Antiphon, Demosthenes, Dinarchus, Hyperides, Isaeus, Isocrates, Lycurgus, and Lysias. This is the fourth volume of Demosthenes; it includes an assortment of relatively little-known works: a funeral oration, an erotic essay, some 55 short prologues, and six letters. In different ways they shed interesting light on Demosthenes' work and the last years of his life.

This volume marks the two-thirds point in the series, and as always, I would like to thank all those at the University of Texas Press who have worked with this and the other volumes in the series: Director Joanna Hitchcock, Humanities Editor Jim Burr, Manuscript Editor Lynne Chapman, and Copyeditor Nancy Moore. I also want to thank Carolyn Wylie, who retired just before this current volume went into copyediting. Carolyn saw the previous nine volumes through production and is responsible for the very high quality this series has attained. She will be missed.

—M. G.

TRANSLATOR'S ACKNOWLEDGMENTS

I am very grateful to Michael Gagarin for the amount of time he spent on an earlier draft of this book and for his myriad suggestions on the translations, all of which were to its and my own benefit: I owe him at least two red pens. I am also indebted to the anonymous referee for many thoughtful suggestions. I consider the person to whom this book is dedicated, Marianne McDonald, one of my closest friends, and I am deeply grateful for her support and encouragement over many years. And as always, I thank my family for its support and for letting me do what I do.

Reviewers please note: Since the aim of this series is to produce accurate translations with explanatory introductions and notes for mostly the student market and the general public, I have had to keep my notes short and to a minimum. For more detailed discussions of stylistic and historical matters, readers should consult the appropriate works (which also cite previous publications) listed in the Bibliography.

—I. W.

SPEECH NUMBERS AND TITLES

This is a list of the orators' speeches cited in this volume by number and title for ease of reference (speeches believed to be spurious but which have survived under the name of a particular orator are cited under that name).

Aeschines
  1 Against Timarchus
  2 On the False Embassy
  3 Against Ctesiphon

Andocides
  1 On the Mysteries

Demosthenes
  1 Olynthiac 1
  3 Olynthiac 3
  4 Philippic 1
  7 On Halonnesus
  8 On the Chersonese
  9 Philippic 3
  10 Philippic 4
  13 On Organization
  14 On the Navy Boards
  15 For the Liberty of the Rhodians
  16 For the People of Megalopolis
  17 On the Treaty with Alexander
  18 On the Crown
  19 On the False Embassy

SERIES INTRODUCTION
Greek Oratory

By Michael Gagarin

ORATORY IN CLASSICAL ATHENS

From as early as Homer (and undoubtedly much earlier) the Greeks placed a high value on effective speaking. Even Achilles, whose greatness was primarily established on the battlefield, was brought up to be "a speaker of words and a doer of deeds" (*Iliad* 9.443); and Athenian leaders of the sixth and fifth centuries,[1] such as Solon, Themistocles, and Pericles, were all accomplished orators. Most Greek literary genres—notably epic, tragedy, and history—underscore the importance of oratory by their inclusion of set speeches. The formal pleadings of the envoys to Achilles in the *Iliad,* the messenger speeches in tragedy reporting events like the battle of Salamis in Aeschylus' *Persians* or the gruesome death of Pentheus in Euripides' *Bacchae,* and the powerful political oratory of Pericles' funeral oration in Thucydides are but a few of the most notable examples of the Greeks' never-ending fascination with formal public speaking, which was to reach its height in the public oratory of the fourth century.

In early times, oratory was not a specialized subject of study but was learned by practice and example. The formal study of rhetoric as an "art" (*technē*) began, we are told, in the middle of the fifth century in Sicily with the work of Corax and his pupil Tisias.[2] These two are

---

[1] All dates in this volume are BC unless the contrary is either indicated or obvious.

[2] See Kennedy 1963: 26–51. Cole 1991 has challenged this traditional picture, arguing that the term "rhetoric" was coined by Plato to designate and denigrate an activity he strongly opposed. Cole's own reconstruction is not without problems,

scarcely more than names to us, but another famous Sicilian, Gorgias of Leontini (ca. 490–390), developed a new style of argument and is reported to have dazzled the Athenians with a speech delivered when he visited Athens in 427. Gorgias initiated the practice, which continued into the early fourth century, of composing speeches for mythical or imaginary occasions. The surviving examples reveal a lively intellectual climate in the late fifth and early fourth centuries, in which oratory served to display new ideas, new forms of expression, and new methods of argument.[3] This tradition of "intellectual" oratory was continued by the fourth-century educator Isocrates and played a large role in later Greek and Roman education.

In addition to this intellectual oratory, at about the same time the practice also began of writing speeches for real occasions in public life, which we may designate "practical" oratory. For centuries Athenians had been delivering speeches in public settings (primarily the courts and the Assembly), but these had always been composed and delivered impromptu, without being written down and thus without being preserved. The practice of writing speeches began in the courts and then expanded to include the Assembly and other settings. Athens was one of the leading cities of Greece in the fifth and fourth centuries, and its political and legal systems depended on direct participation by a large number of citizens; all important decisions were made by these large bodies, and the primary means of influencing these decisions was oratory.[4] Thus, it is not surprising that oratory flourished in Athens,[5] but it may not be immediately obvious why it should be written down.

The pivotal figure in this development was Antiphon, one of the fifth-century intellectuals who are often grouped together under the

---

but he does well to remind us how thoroughly the traditional view of rhetoric depends on one of its most ardent opponents.

[3] Of these only Antiphon's Tetralogies are included in this series. Gorgias' *Helen* and *Palamedes,* Alcidamas' *Odysseus,* and Antisthenes' *Ajax* and *Odysseus* are translated in Gagarin and Woodruff 1995.

[4] Yunis 1996 has a good treatment of political oratory from Pericles to Demosthenes.

[5] All our evidence for practical oratory comes from Athens, with the exception of Isocrates 19, written for a trial in Aegina. Many speeches were undoubtedly delivered in courts and political forums in other Greek cities, but it may be that such speeches were written down only in Athens.

name "Sophists."[6] Like some of the other sophists he contributed to the intellectual oratory of the period, but he also had a strong practical interest in law. At the same time, Antiphon had an aversion to public speaking and did not directly involve himself in legal or political affairs (Thucydides 8.68). However, he began giving general advice to other citizens who were engaged in litigation and were thus expected to address the court themselves. As this practice grew, Antiphon went further, and around 430 he began writing out whole speeches for others to memorize and deliver. Thus began the practice of "logography," which continued through the next century and beyond.[7] Logography particularly appealed to men like Lysias, who were metics, or noncitizen residents of Athens. Since they were not Athenian citizens, they were barred from direct participation in public life, but they could contribute by writing speeches for others.

Antiphon was also the first (to our knowledge) to write down a speech he would himself deliver, writing the speech for his own defense at his trial for treason in 411. His motive was probably to publicize and preserve his views, and others continued this practice of writing down speeches they would themselves deliver in the courts and (more rarely) the Assembly.[8] Finally, one other type of practical oratory was the special tribute delivered on certain important public occasions, the best known of which is the funeral oration. It is convenient to designate these three types of oratory by the terms Aristotle later uses: forensic (for the courts), deliberative (for the Assembly), and epideictic (for display).[9]

---

[6] The term "sophist" was loosely used through the fifth and fourth centuries to designate various intellectuals and orators, but under the influence of Plato, who attacked certain figures under this name, the term is now used of a specific group of thinkers; see Kerferd 1981.

[7] For Antiphon as the first to write speeches, see Photius, *Bibliotheca* 486a7–11 and [Plut.], *Moralia* 832c–d. The latest extant speech can be dated to 320, but we know that at least one orator, Dinarchus, continued the practice after that date.

[8] Unlike forensic speeches, speeches for delivery in the Assembly were usually not composed beforehand in writing, since the speaker could not know exactly when or in what context he would be speaking; see further Trevett 1996.

[9] *Rhetoric* 1.3. Intellectual orations, like Gorgias' *Helen,* do not easily fit into Aristotle's classification. For a fuller (but still brief) introduction to Attic oratory and the orators, see Edwards 1994.

THE ORATORS

In the century from about 420 to 320, dozens—perhaps even hundreds—of now unknown orators and logographers must have composed speeches that are now lost, but only ten of these men were selected for preservation and study by ancient scholars, and only works collected under the names of these ten have been preserved. Some of these works are undoubtedly spurious, though in most cases they are fourth-century works by a different author rather than later "forgeries." Indeed, modern scholars suspect that as many as seven of the speeches attributed to Demosthenes may have been written by Apollodorus, son of Pasion, who is sometimes called "the eleventh orator."[10] Including these speeches among the works of Demosthenes may have been an honest mistake, or perhaps a bookseller felt he could sell more copies of these speeches if they were attributed to a more famous orator.

In alphabetical order the Ten Orators are as follows:[11]

- AESCHINES (ca. 395–ca. 322) rose from obscure origins to become an important Athenian political figure, first an ally, then a bitter enemy of Demosthenes. His three speeches all concern major public issues. The best known of these (Aes. 3) was delivered at the trial in 330, when Demosthenes responded with *On the Crown* (Dem. 18). Aeschines lost the case and was forced to leave Athens and live the rest of his life in exile.

- ANDOCIDES (ca. 440–ca. 390) is best known for his role in the scandal of 415, when just before the departure of the fateful Athenian expedition to Sicily during the Peloponnesian War (431–404), a band of young men mutilated statues of Hermes, and at the same time information was revealed about the secret rites of Demeter. Andocides was exiled but later returned. Two of the four speeches

---

[10] See Trevett 1992.

[11] The Loeb volumes of *Minor Attic Orators* also include the prominent Athenian political figure Demades (ca. 385–319), who was not one of the Ten; but the only speech that has come down to us under his name is a later forgery. It is possible that Demades and other fourth-century politicians who had a high reputation for public speaking did not put any speeches in writing, especially if they rarely spoke in the courts (see above n. 8).

in his name give us a contemporary view of the scandal: one pleads for his return, the other argues against a second period of exile.

◆ ANTIPHON (ca. 480–411), as already noted, wrote forensic speeches for others and only once spoke himself. In 411 he participated in an oligarchic coup by a group of 400, and when the democrats regained power he was tried for treason and executed. His six surviving speeches include three for delivery in court and the three Tetralogies—imaginary intellectual exercises for display or teaching that consist of four speeches each, two on each side. All six of Antiphon's speeches concern homicide, probably because these stood at the beginning of the collection of his works. Fragments of some thirty other speeches cover many different topics.

◆ DEMOSTHENES (384–322) is generally considered the best of the Attic orators. Although his nationalistic message is less highly regarded today, his powerful mastery of and ability to combine many different rhetorical styles continues to impress readers. Demosthenes was still a child when his wealthy father died. The trustees of the estate apparently misappropriated much of it, and when he came of age, he sued them in a series of cases (27–31), regaining some of his fortune and making a name as a powerful speaker. He then wrote speeches for others in a variety of cases, public and private, and for his own use in court (where many cases involved major public issues), and in the Assembly, where he opposed the growing power of Philip of Macedon. The triumph of Philip and his son Alexander the Great eventually put an end to Demosthenes' career. Some sixty speeches have come down under his name, about a third of them of questionable authenticity.

◆ DINARCHUS (ca. 360–ca. 290) was born in Corinth but spent much of his life in Athens as a metic (a noncitizen resident). His public fame came primarily from writing speeches for the prosecutions surrounding the Harpalus affair in 324, when several prominent figures (including Demosthenes) were accused of bribery. After 322 he had a profitable career as a logographer.

◆ HYPERIDES (389/8–322) was a political leader and logographer of so many different talents that he was called the pentathlete of orators. He was a leader of the Athenian resistance to Philip and

Alexander and (like Demosthenes) was condemned to death after Athens' final surrender. One speech and substantial fragments of five others have been recovered from papyrus remains; otherwise, only fragments survive.

• ISAEUS (ca. 415–ca. 340) wrote speeches on a wide range of topics, but the eleven complete speeches that survive, dating from ca. 390 to ca. 344, all concern inheritance. As with Antiphon, the survival of these particular speeches may have been the result of the later ordering of his speeches by subject; we have part of a twelfth speech and fragments and titles of some forty other works. Isaeus is said to have been a pupil of Isocrates and the teacher of Demosthenes.

• ISOCRATES (436–338) considered himself a philosopher and educator, not an orator or rhetorician. He came from a wealthy Athenian family but lost most of his property in the Peloponnesian War, and in 403 he took up logography. About 390 he abandoned this practice and turned to writing and teaching, setting forth his educational, philosophical, and political views in essays that took the form of speeches but were not meant for oral delivery. He favored accommodation with the growing power of Philip of Macedon and panhellenic unity. His school was based on a broad concept of rhetoric and applied philosophy; it attracted pupils from the entire Greek world (including Isaeus, Lycurgus, and Hyperides) and became the main rival of Plato's Academy. Isocrates greatly influenced education and rhetoric in the Hellenistic, Roman, and modern periods until the eighteenth century.

• LYCURGUS (ca. 390–ca. 324) was a leading public official who restored the financial condition of Athens after 338 and played a large role in the city for the next dozen years. He brought charges of corruption or treason against many other officials, usually with success. Only one speech survives.

• LYSIAS (ca. 445–ca. 380) was a metic—an official resident of Athens but not a citizen. Much of his property was seized by the Thirty during their short-lived oligarchic coup in 404–403. Perhaps as a result he turned to logography. More than thirty speeches survive in whole or in part, though the authenticity of some is doubted. We also have fragments or know the titles of more than a hundred others. The speeches cover a wide range of cases, and he may have delivered one himself (Lys. 12), on the death of his brother at the hands of the Thirty. Lysias is particularly known for his vivid narratives, his *ēthopoiïa,* or "creation of character," and his prose style, which became a model of clarity and vividness.

THE WORKS OF THE ORATORS

As soon as speeches began to be written down, they could be preserved. We know little about the conditions of book "publication" (i.e., making copies for distribution) in the fourth century, but there was an active market for books in Athens, and some of the speeches may have achieved wide circulation.[12] An orator (or his family) may have preserved his own speeches, perhaps to advertise his ability or demonstrate his success, or booksellers may have collected and copied them in order to make money.

We do not know how closely the preserved text of these speeches corresponded to the version actually delivered in court or in the Assembly. Speakers undoubtedly extemporized or varied from their text on occasion, but there is no good evidence that deliberative speeches were substantially revised for publication.[13] In forensic oratory a logographer's reputation would derive first and foremost from his success with jurors. If a forensic speech was victorious, there would be no reason to alter it for publication, and if it lost, alteration would probably not deceive potential clients. Thus, the published texts of forensic speeches were probably quite faithful to the texts that were provided to clients, and we have little reason to suspect substantial alteration in the century or so before they were collected by scholars in Alexandria (see below).

In addition to the speaker's text, most forensic speeches have breaks for the inclusion of documents. The logographer inserted a notation in his text—such as *nomos* ("law") or *martyria* ("testimony")—and the

---

[12] Dover's discussion (1968) of the preservation and transmission of the works of Lysias (and perhaps others under his name) is useful not just for Lysias but for the other orators too. His theory of shared authorship between logographer and litigant, however, is unconvincing (see Usher 1976).

[13] See further Trevett 1996: 437–439.

speaker would pause while the clerk read out the text of a law or the testimony of witnesses. Many speeches survive with only a notation that a *nomos* or *martyria* was read at that point, but in some cases the text of the document is included. It used to be thought that these documents were all creations of later scholars, but many (though not all) are now accepted as genuine.[14]

With the foundation of the famous library in Alexandria early in the third century, scholars began to collect and catalogue texts of the orators, along with many other classical authors. Only the best orators were preserved in the library, many of them represented by over 100 speeches each (some undoubtedly spurious). Only some of these works survived in manuscript form to the modern era; more recently a few others have been discovered on ancient sheets of papyrus, so that today the corpus of Attic Oratory consists of about 150 speeches, together with a few letters and other works. The subject matter ranges from important public issues and serious crimes to business affairs, lovers' quarrels, inheritance disputes, and other personal or family matters.

In the centuries after these works were collected, ancient scholars gathered biographical facts about their authors, produced grammatical and lexicographic notes, and used some of the speeches as evidence for Athenian political history. But the ancient scholars who were most interested in the orators were those who studied prose style, the most notable of these being Dionysius of Halicarnassus (first century BC), who wrote treatises on several of the orators,[15] and Hermogenes of Tarsus (second century AD), who wrote several literary studies, including *On Types of Style*.[16] But relative to epic or tragedy, oratory was little studied; and even scholars of rhetoric whose interests were broader than style, like Cicero and Quintilian, paid little attention to the orators, except for the acknowledged master, Demosthenes.

Most modern scholars until the second half of the twentieth century continued to treat the orators primarily as prose stylists.[17] The

---

[14] See MacDowell 1990: 43–47; Todd 1993: 44–45.

[15] Dionysius' literary studies are collected and translated in Usher 1974–1985.

[16] Wooten 1987. Stylistic considerations probably also influenced the selection of the "canon" of ten orators; see Worthington 1994.

[17] For example, the most popular and influential book ever written on the orators, Jebb's *The Attic Orators* (1875) was presented as an "attempt to aid in giving Attic Oratory its due place in the history of Attic Prose" (I.xiii). This modern focus

reevaluation of Athenian democracy by George Grote and others in the nineteenth century stimulated renewed interest in Greek oratory among historians; and increasing interest in Athenian law during that century led a few legal scholars to read the orators. But in comparison with the interest shown in the other literary genres—epic, lyric, tragedy, comedy, and even history—Attic oratory has been relatively neglected until the last third of the twentieth century. More recently, however, scholars have discovered the value of the orators for the broader study of Athenian culture and society. Since Dover's groundbreaking works on popular morality and homosexuality,[18] interest in the orators has been increasing rapidly, and they are now seen as primary representatives of Athenian moral and social values, and as evidence for social and economic conditions, political and social ideology, and in general those aspects of Athenian culture that in the past were commonly ignored by historians of ancient Greece but are of increasing interest and importance today, including women and the family, slavery, and the economy.

GOVERNMENT AND LAW IN CLASSICAL ATHENS

The hallmark of the Athenian political and legal systems was its amateurism. Most public officials, including those who supervised the courts, were selected by lot and held office for a limited period, typically a year. Thus a great many citizens held public office at some point in their lives, but almost none served for an extended period of time or developed the experience or expertise that would make them professionals. All significant policy decisions were debated and voted on in the Assembly, where the quorum was 6,000 citizens, and all significant legal cases were judged by bodies of 200 to 500 jurors or more. Public prominence was not achieved by election (or selection) to public office but depended rather on a man's ability to sway the majority of citizens in the Assembly or jurors in court to vote in favor of a pro-

---

on prose style can plausibly be connected to the large role played by prose composition (the translation of English prose into Greek, usually in imitation of specific authors or styles) in the Classics curriculum, especially in Britain.

[18] Dover (1974, 1978). Dover recently commented (1994: 157), "When I began to mine the riches of Attic forensic oratory I was astonished to discover that the mine had never been exploited."

posed course of action or for one of the litigants in a trial. Success was
never permanent, and a victory on one policy issue or a verdict in one
case could be quickly reversed in another.[19] In such a system the value
of public oratory is obvious, and in the fourth century, oratory became
the most important cultural institution in Athens, replacing drama
as the forum where major ideological concerns were displayed and
debated.

Several recent books give good detailed accounts of Athenian government and law,[20] and so a brief sketch can suffice here. The main
policy-making body was the Assembly, open to all adult male citizens;
a small payment for attendance enabled at least some of the poor to
attend along with the leisured rich. In addition, a Council of 500 citizens, selected each year by lot with no one allowed to serve more than
two years, prepared material for and made recommendations to the
Assembly; a rotating subgroup of this Council served as an executive
committee, the Prytaneis. Finally, numerous officials, most of them
selected by lot for one-year terms, supervised different areas of administration and finance. The most important of these were the nine Archons (lit. "rulers"): the eponymous Archon after whom the year was
named, the Basileus ("king"),[21] the Polemarch, and the six Thesmo-
thetae. Councilors and almost all these officials underwent a preliminary examination (*dokimasia*) before taking office, and officials sub-
mitted to a final accounting (*euthynai*) upon leaving; at these times
any citizen who wished could challenge a person's fitness for his new
position or his performance in his recent position.

---

[19] In the Assembly this could be accomplished by a reconsideration of the
question, as in the famous Mytilenean debate (Thuc. 3.36–50); in court a verdict
was final, but its practical effects could be thwarted or reversed by later litigation
on a related issue.

[20] For government, see Sinclair 1988, Hansen 1991; for law, MacDowell 1978,
Todd 1993, and Boegehold 1995 (Bonner 1927 is still helpful). Much of our information about the legal and political systems comes from a work attributed to
Aristotle but perhaps written by a pupil of his, *The Athenian Constitution* (*Ath.
Pol.*—conveniently translated with notes by Rhodes 1984). The discovery of this
work on a papyrus in Egypt in 1890 caused a major resurgence of interest in Athenian government.

[21] Modern scholars often use the term *archōn basileus* or "king archon," but
Athenian sources (e.g., *Ath. Pol.* 57) simply call him the *basileus*.

There was no general taxation of Athenian citizens. Sources of public funding included the annual tax levied on metics, various fees and import duties, and (in the fifth century) tribute from allied cities; but the source that figures most prominently in the orators is the Athenian system of liturgies (*leitourgiai*), by which in a regular rotation the rich provided funding for certain special public needs. The main liturgies were the *chorēgia*, in which a sponsor (*chorēgos*) supervised and paid for the training and performance of a chorus which sang and danced at a public festival,[22] and the trierarchy, in which a sponsor (trierarch) paid to equip and usually commanded a trireme, or warship, for a year. Some of these liturgies required substantial expenditures, but even so, some men spent far more than required in order to promote themselves and their public careers, and litigants often tried to impress the jurors by referring to liturgies they had undertaken (see, e.g., Lys. 21.1–n5). A further twist on this system was that if a man thought he had been assigned a liturgy that should have gone to someone else who was richer than he, he could propose an exchange of property (*antidosis*), giving the other man a choice of either taking over the liturgy or exchanging property with him. Finally, the rich were also subject to special taxes (*eisphorai*) levied as a percentage of their property in times of need.

The Athenian legal system remained similarly resistant to professionalization. Trials and the procedures leading up to them were supervised by officials, primarily the nine Archons, but their role was purely administrative, and they were in no way equivalent to modern judges. All significant questions about what we would call points of law were presented to the jurors, who considered them together with all other issues when they delivered their verdict at the end of the trial.[23] Trials were "contests" (*agōnes*) between two litigants, each of whom presented his own case to the jurors in a speech, plaintiff first, then de-

---

[22] These included the productions of tragedy and comedy, for which the main expense was for the chorus.

[23] Certain religious "interpreters" (*exēgētai*) were occasionally asked to give their opinion on a legal matter that had a religious dimension (such as the prosecution of a homicide), but although these opinions could be reported in court (e.g., Dem. 47.68–73), they had no official legal standing. The most significant administrative decision we hear of is the refusal of the Basileus to accept the case in Antiphon 6 (see 6.37–46).

fendant; in some cases each party then spoke again, probably in rebuttal. Since a litigant had only one or two speeches in which to present his entire case, and no issue was decided separately by a judge, all the necessary factual information and every important argument on substance or procedure, fact or law, had to be presented together. A single speech might thus combine narrative, argument, emotional appeal, and various digressions, all with the goal of obtaining a favorable verdict. Even more than today, a litigant's primary task was to control the issue—to determine which issues the jurors would consider most important and which questions they would have in their minds as they cast their votes. We only rarely have both speeches from a trial,[24] and we usually have little or no external evidence for the facts of a case or the verdict. We must thus infer both the facts and the opponent's strategy from the speech we have, and any assessment of the overall effectiveness of a speech and of the logographer's strategy is to some extent speculative.

Before a trial there were usually several preliminary hearings for presenting evidence; arbitration, public and private, was available and sometimes required. These hearings and arbitration sessions allowed each side to become familiar with the other side's case, so that discussions of "what my opponent will say" could be included in one's speech. Normally a litigant presented his own case, but he was often assisted by family or friends. If he wished (and could afford it), he could enlist the services of a logographer, who presumably gave strategic advice in addition to writing a speech. The speeches were timed to ensure an equal hearing for both sides,[25] and all trials were completed within a day. Two hundred or more jurors decided each case in the popular courts, which met in the Agora.[26] Homicide cases and certain other religious trials (e.g., Lys. 7) were heard by the Council of the Areopagus or an associated group of fifty-one Ephetae. The Areopagus was composed of all former Archons—perhaps 150–200 members at most

---

[24] The exceptions are Demosthenes 19 and Aeschines 2, Aeschines 3 and Demosthenes 18, and Lysias 6 (one of several prosecution speeches) and Andocides 1; all were written for major public cases.

[25] Timing was done by means of a water-clock, which in most cases was stopped during the reading of documents.

[26] See Boegehold 1995.

times. It met on a hill called the Areopagus ("rock of Ares") near the Acropolis.

Jurors for the regular courts were selected by lot from those citizens who registered each year and who appeared for duty that day; as with the Assembly, a small payment allowed the poor to serve. After the speakers had finished, the jurors voted immediately without any formal discussion. The side with the majority won; a tie vote decided the case for the defendant. In some cases where the penalty was not fixed, after a conviction the jurors voted again on the penalty, choosing between penalties proposed by each side. Even when we know the verdict, we cannot know which of the speaker's arguments contributed most to his success or failure. However, a logographer could probably learn from jurors which points had or had not been successful, so that arguments that are found repeatedly in speeches probably were known to be effective in most cases.

The first written laws in Athens were enacted by Draco (ca. 620) and Solon (ca. 590), and new laws were regularly added. At the end of the fifth century the existing laws were reorganized, and a new procedure for enacting laws was instituted; thereafter a group of Law-Givers (*nomothetai*) had to certify that a proposed law did not conflict with any existing laws. There was no attempt, however, to organize legislation systematically, and although Plato, Aristotle, and other philosophers wrote various works on law and law-giving, these were either theoretical or descriptive and had no apparent influence on legislation. Written statutes generally used ordinary language rather than precise legal definitions in designating offenses, and questions concerning precisely what constituted a specific offense or what was the correct interpretation of a written statute were decided (together with other issues) by the jurors in each case. A litigant might, of course, assert a certain definition or interpretation as "something you all know" or "what the lawgiver intended," but such remarks are evidently tendentious and cannot be taken as authoritative.

The result of these procedural and substantive features was that the verdict depended largely on each litigant's speech (or speeches). As one speaker puts it (Ant. 6.18), "When there are no witnesses, you (jurors) are forced to reach a verdict about the case on the basis of the prosecutor's and defendant's words alone; you must be suspicious and examine their accounts in detail, and your vote will necessarily be cast on the basis of likelihood rather than clear knowledge." Even the testimony of witnesses (usually on both sides) is rarely decisive. On the other hand, most speakers make a considerable effort to establish facts and provide legitimate arguments in conformity with established law. Plato's view of rhetoric as a clever technique for persuading an ignorant crowd that the false is true is not borne out by the speeches, and the legal system does not appear to have produced many arbitrary or clearly unjust results.

The main form of legal procedure was a *dikē* ("suit") in which the injured party (or his relatives in a case of homicide) brought suit against the offender. Suits for injuries to slaves would be brought by the slave's master, and injuries to women would be prosecuted by a male relative. Strictly speaking, a *dikē* was a private matter between individuals, though like all cases, *dikai* often had public dimensions. The other major form of procedure was a *graphē* ("writing" or "indictment") in which "anyone who wished" (i.e., any citizen) could bring a prosecution for wrongdoing. *Graphai* were instituted by Solon, probably in order to allow prosecution of offenses where the victim was unable or unlikely to bring suit himself, such as selling a dependent into slavery; but the number of areas covered by *graphai* increased to cover many types of public offenses as well as some apparently private crimes, such as *hybris*.

The system of prosecution by "anyone who wished" also extended to several other more specialized forms of prosecution, like *eisangelia* ("impeachment"), used in cases of treason. Another specialized prosecution was *apagōgē* ("summary arrest"), in which someone could arrest a common criminal (*kakourgos*, lit. "evil-doer"), or have him arrested, on the spot. The reliance on private initiative meant that Athenians never developed a system of public prosecution; rather, they presumed that everyone would keep an eye on the behavior of his political enemies and bring suit as soon as he suspected a crime, both to harm his opponents and to advance his own career. In this way all public officials would be watched by someone. There was no disgrace in admitting that a prosecution was motivated by private enmity.

By the end of the fifth century the system of prosecution by "anyone who wished" was apparently being abused by so-called sykophants (*sykophantai*), who allegedly brought or threatened to bring false suits against rich men, either to gain part of the fine that would be levied or to induce an out-of-court settlement in which the accused would pay to have the matter dropped. We cannot gauge the true extent of this problem, since speakers usually provide little evidence to support their claims that their opponents are sykophants, but the Athenians did make sykophancy a crime. They also specified that in many public procedures a plaintiff who either dropped the case or failed to obtain one-fifth of the votes would have to pay a heavy fine of 1,000 drachmas. Despite this, it appears that litigation was common in Athens and was seen by some as excessive.

Over the course of time, the Athenian legal and political systems have more often been judged negatively than positively. Philosophers and political theorists have generally followed the lead of Plato (427–347), who lived and worked in Athens his entire life while severely criticizing its system of government as well as many other aspects of its culture. For Plato, democracy amounted to the tyranny of the masses over the educated elite and was destined to collapse from its own instability. The legal system was capricious and depended entirely on the rhetorical ability of litigants with no regard for truth or justice. These criticisms have often been echoed by modern scholars, who particularly complain that law was much too closely interwoven with politics and did not have the autonomous status it achieved in Roman law and continues to have, at least in theory, in modern legal systems.

Plato's judgments are valid if one accepts the underlying presuppositions, that the aim of law is absolute truth and abstract justice and that achieving the highest good of the state requires thorough and systematic organization. Most Athenians do not seem to have subscribed to either the criticisms or the presuppositions, and most scholars now accept the long-ignored fact that despite major external disruptions in the form of wars and two short-lived coups brought about by one of these wars, the Athenian legal and political systems remained remarkably stable for almost two hundred years (508–320). Moreover, like all other Greek cities at the time, whatever their form of government, Athenian democracy was brought to an end not by internal forces but by the external power of Philip of Macedon and his son Alexander. The legal system never became autonomous, and the rich sometimes complained that they were victims of unscrupulous litigants, but there is no indication that the people wanted to yield control of the legal process to a professional class, as Plato recommended. For most Athenians—Plato being an exception in this and many other matters—one purpose of the legal system was to give everyone the opportunity to have his case heard by other citizens and have it heard quickly and cheaply; and in this it clearly succeeded.

Indeed, the Athenian legal system also served the interests of the rich, even the very rich, as well as the common people, in that it provided a forum for the competition that since Homer had been an important part of aristocratic life. In this competition, the rich used the courts as battlegrounds, though their main weapon was the rhetoric of popular ideology, which hailed the rule of law and promoted the ideal of moderation and restraint.[27] But those who aspired to political leadership and the honor and status that accompanied it repeatedly entered the legal arena, bringing suit against their political enemies whenever possible and defending themselves against suits brought by others whenever necessary. The ultimate judges of these public competitions were the common people, who seem to have relished the dramatic clash of individuals and ideologies. In this respect fourth-century oratory was the cultural heir of fifth-century drama and was similarly appreciated by the citizens. Despite the disapproval of intellectuals like Plato, most Athenians legitimately considered their legal system a hallmark of their democracy and a vital presence in their culture.

THE TRANSLATION OF GREEK ORATORY

The purpose of this series is to provide students and scholars in all fields with accurate, readable translations of all surviving classical Attic oratory, including speeches whose authenticity is disputed, as well as the substantial surviving fragments. In keeping with the originals, the language is for the most part nontechnical. Names of persons and places are given in the (generally more familiar) Latinized forms, and names of officials or legal procedures have been translated into English equivalents, where possible. Notes are intended to provide the necessary historical and cultural background; scholarly controversies are generally not discussed. The notes and introductions refer to scholarly treatments in addition to those listed below, which the reader may consult for further information.

---

[27] Ober 1989 is fundamental; see also Cohen 1995.

Cross-references to other speeches follow the standard numbering system, which is now well established except in the case of Hyperides (for whom the numbering of the Oxford Classical Text is used).[28] References are by work and section (e.g., Dem. 24.73); spurious works are not specially marked; when no author is named (e.g., 24.73), the reference is to the same author as the annotated passage.

ABBREVIATIONS

Aes.	=	Aeschines
And.	=	Andocides
Ant.	=	Antiphon
Arist.	=	Aristotle
Aristoph.	=	Aristophanes
Ath. Pol.	=	*The Athenian Constitution*
Dem.	=	Demosthenes
Din.	=	Dinarchus
Herod.	=	Herodotus
Hyp.	=	Hyperides
Is.	=	Isaeus
Isoc.	=	Isocrates
Lyc.	=	Lycurgus
Lys.	=	Lysias
Plut.	=	Plutarch
Thuc.	=	Thucydides
Xen.	=	Xenophon

NOTE: The main unit of Athenian currency was the drachma; this was divided into obols and larger amounts were designated minas and talents.

1 drachma	=	6 obols
1 mina	=	100 drachmas
1 talent	=	60 minas (6,000 drachmas)

It is impossible to give an accurate equivalence in terms of modern currency, but it may be helpful to remember that the daily wage of

---

[28] For a listing of all the orators and their works, with classifications (forensic, deliberative, epideictic) and rough dates, see Edwards 1994: 74–79.

some skilled workers was a drachma in the mid-fifth century and 2–
2½ drachmas in the later fourth century. Thus it may not be too misleading to think of a drachma as worth about $50 or £33 and a talent
as about $300,000 or £200,000 in 1997 currency.

BIBLIOGRAPHY OF WORKS CITED

Boegehold, Alan L., 1995: *The Lawcourts at Athens: Sites, Buildings,
Equipment, Procedure, and Testimonia.* Princeton.
Bonner, Robert J., 1927: *Lawyers and Litigants in Ancient Athens.*
Chicago.
Carey, Christopher, 1997: *Trials from Classical Athens.* London.
Cohen, David, 1995: *Law, Violence and Community in Classical Athens.*
Cambridge.
Cole, Thomas, 1991: *The Origins of Rhetoric in Ancient Greece.*
Baltimore.
Dover, Kenneth J., 1968: *Lysias and the Corpus Lysiacum.* Berkeley.
———, 1974: *Greek Popular Morality in the Time of Plato and Aris-
totle.* Oxford.
———, 1978: *Greek Homosexuality.* London.
———, 1994: *Marginal Comment.* London.
Edwards, Michael, 1994: *The Attic Orators.* London.
Gagarin, Michael, and Paul Woodruff, 1995: *Early Greek Political
Thought from Homer to the Sophists.* Cambridge.
Hansen, Mogens Herman, 1991: *The Athenian Democracy in the Age of
Demosthenes.* Oxford.
Jebb, Richard, 1875: *The Attic Orators,* 2 vols. London.
Kennedy, George A., 1963: *The Art of Persuasion in Greece.* Princeton.
Kerferd, G. B., 1981: *The Sophistic Movement.* Cambridge.
MacDowell, Douglas M., 1978: *The Law in Classical Athens.* London.
———, ed. 1990: *Demosthenes, Against Meidias.* Oxford.
Ober, Josiah, 1989: *Mass and Elite in Democratic Athens.* Princeton.
Rhodes, P. J., trans., 1984: *Aristotle, The Athenian Constitution.* Penguin
Books.
Sinclair, R. K., 1988: *Democracy and Participation in Athens.* Cam-
bridge.
Todd, Stephen, 1993: *The Shape of Athenian Law.* Oxford.

Trevett, Jeremy, 1992: *Apollodoros the Son of Pasion.* Oxford.

————, 1996: "Did Demosthenes Publish His Deliberative Speeches?" *Hermes* 124: 425–441.

Usher, Stephen, 1976: "Lysias and His Clients," *Greek, Roman and Byzantine Studies* 17: 31–40.

————, trans., 1974–1985: *Dionysius of Halicarnassus, Critical Essays.* 2 vols. Loeb Classical Library. Cambridge, MA.

————, 1999: *Greek Oratory: Tradition and Originality.* Oxford.

Wooten, Cecil W., trans., 1987: *Hermogenes' On Types of Style.* Chapel Hill, NC.

Worthington, Ian, 1994: "The Canon of the Ten Attic Orators," in *Persuasion: Greek Rhetoric in Action,* ed. Ian Worthington. London: 244–263.

Yunis, Harvey, 1996: *Taming Democracy: Models of Political Rhetoric in Classical Athens.* Ithaca, NY.

DEMOSTHENES, SPEECHES 60 AND 61,
PROLOGUES, LETTERS

INTRODUCTION TO DEMOSTHENES

By Michael Gagarin

Since antiquity Demosthenes (384–322 BC) has usually been judged the greatest of the Attic orators. Although the patriotic and nationalistic tenor of his message has been more highly regarded in some periods of history than in others, he is unique in his mastery of so many different rhetorical styles and his ability to blend them into a powerful ensemble.

LIFE

Demosthenes was born into an old wealthy Athenian family. His father Demosthenes owned workshops that made swords and furniture. His maternal grandfather, Gylon, had been exiled from Athens and lived in the Crimea, where his mother Cleobule was born (perhaps to a Scythian mother). When Demosthenes was seven, his father died leaving his estate in the trust of several guardians. According to Demosthenes' own account, the guardians mismanaged and defrauded the estate to the point that when he turned eighteen, the age of majority, he received almost nothing. He devoted the next several years to recovering his property, first studying forensic pleading and then bringing a series of suits against the guardians to recover his patrimony (speeches 27–31). He won the first case (27, *Against Aphobus I*), but then had to bring several more suits in order to collect the amount awarded him by the court. In the course of these trials he gained a reputation as a successful speaker, became sought after by others, and began to write speeches for a wide range of private suits, including inheritance, shipping loans, assault, and trespass. His clients included one of the richest men in Athens, the banker Phormio; the speech *For Phormio* (36) involves a dispute over twenty talents (equivalent to several million dollars today). Demosthenes' vivid characterization of the honest, hard-working Phormio and his malicious and extravagant opponent proved so convincing that the jurors reportedly refused to listen to the other side and took the highly unusual step of voting immediately for Phormio.

In 355 Demosthenes became involved in his first major public case (22, *Against Androtion*). By this time it was common for ambitious or influential citizens to bring legal charges against their political opponents on matters of public interest. Charges of proposing an illegal decree (the *graphē paranomōn*) were particularly common; these involved the indictment of the proposer of a decree on the ground that it conflicted with existing law.[1] Although these speeches addressed the specific issue of a conflict between laws, it was generally accepted that the merits of the decree, and of its proposer, were also relevant factors, and these cases formed a major arena for the ongoing political struggles between leading figures in the city.

About the same time Demosthenes also began to publish speeches on public issues which he delivered in the assembly, and after 350, although he continued from time to time to write speeches for private disputes, he turned his attention primarily to public policy, especially relations between Athens and the growing power of Macedon under King Philip. Demosthenes' strategy throughout was to increase Athens' military readiness, to oppose Philip's expansion and to support other Greek cities in their resistance to it. Most notable in support of these objectives were the three *Olynthiacs* (1–3) in 349 unsuccessfully urging support for the city of Olynthus (which soon afterwards fell to Philip) and the four *Philippics* (4, 6, 9, 10) in 351–341 urging greater opposition to Philip. But Philip continued to extend his power into Greece, and in 338 he defeated a combined Greek force (including Athens) at the battle of Chaeronea in Boeotia, north of Attica. This battle

---

[1] One might compare the U.S. procedure of challenging the constitutionality of a law in court. Differences include the fact that today no charge is brought against the proposer of the law and that the case is heard by a small panel of professional judges, not the hundreds of untrained jurors who would have heard the case in Athens.

is usually taken to mark the end of the Greek cities' struggle to remain independent.

After Chaeronea Demosthenes continued to urge resistance to Philip, but his efforts were largely ineffectual and his successes and failures are more a matter of internal Athenian politics. His most prominent opponent during this period was Aeschines, who had been acquitted earlier (343) when Demosthenes brought a suit against him in connection with a delegation to Philip on which both men had served (19, cf. Aeschines 2). After Chaeronea, when a minor ally of Demosthenes named Ctesiphon proposed a decree awarding a crown to Demosthenes in recognition of his service to the city, Aeschines brought a *graphē paranomōn* against Ctesiphon (Aeschines 3). The suit, which was not tried until 330, raised legal objections to the proposed decree but also attacked the person and career of Demosthenes at considerable length. Demosthenes responded with his most famous speech *On the Crown* (18), often known by its Latin name *De Corona*. The verdict was so one-sided that Aeschines was fined for not receiving one-fifth of the votes and went into exile. This was Demosthenes' greatest triumph. The last years of his life, however, resulted in notable defeats, first in the rather shadowy Harpalus affair (324–323), from which no speech of his survives (but see Dinarchus 1). Shortly afterwards he was condemned to death at the instigation of pro-Macedonian forces and committed suicide.

WORKS

Sixty-one speeches and some miscellaneous works, including a collection of letters, have come down to us under Demosthenes' name. The authenticity of many of these has been challenged, often because of the allegedly poor quality of the work; but this reason is less often accepted today, and most of the public speeches and many of the private speeches are now thought to be authentic. Among the main exceptions are a group of private speeches (45, 46, 49, 50, 52, 53, 59 and possibly 47 and 51) that were delivered by Apollodorus and are now commonly thought to have been composed by him (Trevett 1992).

Apart from a funeral oration (60) and collections of proems and letters, Demosthenes' works fall into two groups, the assembly speeches (1–17) and the court speeches (18–59); the latter can be further divided into public and private speeches, though these are not formal legal categories. Notable among the public forensic speeches are *Against Meidias* (21), which has recently drawn attention for its pronouncements on Athenian public values, and his last surviving speech, *On the Crown* (18), generally recognized as his masterpiece. In this speech he uses his entire repertory of rhetorical strategies to defend his life and political career. He treats the legal issues of the case briefly, as being of minor concern, and then defends his conduct during the past three decades of Athenian history, arguing that even when his policy did not succeed, on each occasion it was the best policy for the city, in contrast to Aeschines' policies, which, when he ventured to propose any, were disastrous. Demosthenes' extensive personal attack on Aeschines' life and family may be too harsh for modern taste, but the blending of facts, innuendoes, sarcasm, rhetorical questions, and other devices is undeniably effective.

Demosthenes' private speeches have recently begun to attract more interest from scholars, who draw from them insight into Athenian social, political, and economic life. Only the speeches concerned with recovering his inheritance (27–31) were delivered by Demosthenes himself; the rest were written for delivery by other litigants. We have already noted *For Phormio,* which is one of several having to do with banking. *Against Conon* (54) alleges an assault by several young rowdies spurred on by their father, and *Against Neaera* (59), delivered and probably written by Apollodorus, recounts the life of a former slave woman and her affairs with different Athenian men.

STYLE

Demosthenes is a master of Greek prose style; he paid careful attention to style, and to the oral delivery of his speeches. His Roman counterpart, Cicero, modeled his oratorical style (and some other features of his work) in part on Demosthenes' Greek. Although Demosthenes' style varied considerably over the course of time and among the different types of speeches, later assessments of his style are based primarily on the public forensic speeches, and especially the last of these, *On the Crown.* Long and sometimes elaborate sentences are one feature of his style, but Demosthenes' true greatness is his ability to write in many styles and to vary his style, mixing different features together both to suit the topic and to give variety and vigor to his speeches. The final product required great skill and practice to deliver effectively, and the stories about Demosthenes' rigorous training in delivery (see in general Plutarch, *Life of Demosthenes* 6–7), even if not literally true, accurately reflect his priorities. Indeed, only by reading aloud sections of *On the Crown* in Greek can one truly appreciate the power and authority of his prose.

SIGNIFICANCE

Demosthenes played a vital role in Athenian public affairs for some thirty years. His advocacy of the vigilant defense of Greece against foreign invaders, though ultimately unsuccessful in preserving Greek freedom, inspired his fellow Athenians with patriotic loyalty, and has similarly inspired many others in later times. In recent times political rhetoric has not been so widely admired as in the past, and Demosthenes is less read today than he used to be. But he still represents the greatest achievement of Greek oratory and stands as one of the greatest orators of any age.

INTRODUCTION TO THIS VOLUME

By Ian Worthington

THE WORKS IN THIS VOLUME

Contained herein are the *Funeral Oration* (*epitaphios*) for those who died in the Battle of Chaeronea in 338 (60), the *Erotic Essay*, of unknown date (61), 56 (or, rather, 55)[1] *Prologues* (*prooimia*) or openings of political speeches, also of unknown date, and six *Letters*, apparently written during Demosthenes' exile (323 to 322) for his part in the Harpalus affair of 324/3. All of these works are grouped together at the end of the Demosthenic corpus since it was common practice by ancient compilers to place such works at the end of a corpus. The only important studies of them in virtually the past century are the three Budé editions of R. Clavaud and J. Goldstein's *The Letters of Demosthenes* (see below).

The neglect is because of two main reasons: first, scholarly attention has focused on Demosthenes' forensic and political speeches, and second, problems of authenticity. The lack of attention, however, has caused a major gap in Demosthenic scholarship, for their value as sources of information on history, society, and politics, as well as on Demosthenes' rhetorical style, will be evident from reading them. Furthermore, the *Funeral Oration* (*epitaphios*), *Prologues*, and five of the six *Letters* are probably genuine (some discussion of their authorship and dates are given in my introductions). Thus, it is my contention that these works should no longer be relegated to mere passing mention in any discussion of Demosthenes.

---

[1] Only 55 of these are actual prologues, as Number 54 is an account of state sacrifices performed in order to protect the city's safety.

HISTORICAL BACKGROUND TO THE
FUNERAL ORATION AND *LETTERS*

The contemporary literary sources of information for Greece in the 330s and 320s are the speeches of the orators Aeschines, Demosthenes, Dinarchus, Hyperides, and Lycurgus. However, they have their pitfalls. Speeches are not historical but rhetorical works, hence their information has to be treated carefully. The orators were out to win their cases (whether in a lawcourt or an Assembly debate), and accuracy of content mattered less than persuasive presentation.[2] Demosthenes has an axe to grind in the *Funeral Oration* and especially the *Letters,* in which his aim is to be recalled from a self-imposed exile. In order to understand them more fully, it is necessary to be aware of some historical background.

Demosthenes' political influence in Athens was so great that in 340 he easily persuaded the Athenians to declare war on Philip II, king of Macedonia, who by then wanted to reduce Greece. The war did not last long. Despite some initial reversals for the Macedonian king, in 338 Athens and Thebes, helped by several other states (Dem. 18.237), fought him at Chaeronea in Boeotia on 1 September. At stake for the Greeks was their autonomy; for Philip, Macedonian hegemony over Greece.

The Greeks put together an army of 35,000 infantry and 1,400 cavalry to battle Philip's force of 30,000 infantry and 2,000 cavalry (Diodorus Siculus 16.85). Thanks to brilliant strategy, Philip lulled the Athenian contingent into thinking he was retreating, causing the Athenians to rush forward and open the allied line of defense. Alexander, heir to the throne and in charge of the left flank, seized the opportunity to penetrate the Athenian contingent with his cavalry while Philip counter-charged. The young heir was also responsible for annihilating the 300-strong Sacred Band of Thebes. Thus, the battle ended in a Greek rout.[3]

Philip treated the majority of his Greek opponents harshly, estab-

---

[2] See further Worthington 1994b, pp. 109–129.

[3] On the battle, see Diodorus Siculus 16.85.5–86.6; Plut., *Alexander* 9; and for modern discussions, see Hammond and Griffith 1979, pp. 596–603.

lishing oligarchies and garrisons in several cities. The Athenians expected him to march on their city (Lyc. 1.39–45), and Demosthenes and Hyperides proposed a series of emergency measures.[4] Demosthenes prudently left Athens on the pretext of securing grain,[5] for which Dinarchus, for example, later condemned him (cf. 1.80–81).[6] Philip did not, however, besiege Athens. He ordered the Athenians to disband their Second Athenian Naval Confederacy, an empire founded almost half a century earlier in 378.[7] Then he returned the Athenian prisoners captured at Chaeronea unransomed, and Alexander and Antipater escorted the ashes of those who died there to Athens.[8] The democratic institutions of the city were left untouched, and no demand was made for the surrender of anti-Macedonian politicians such as Demosthenes and Hyperides.

Not long after the Battle of Chaeronea,[9] but clearly after he had returned from his mission to secure grain, Demosthenes was chosen by the Athenians to deliver the funeral oration over those who had died in the battle (Dem. 18.285; Plut., *Demosthenes* 21.2). It was the custom of the Athenians to honor their dead in a solemn public ceremony, which was held in the Ceramicus district of Athens, and for a leading statesman to deliver a funeral oration (Thuc. 2.34). The ceremony was customarily attended by citizens and metics (noncitizen residents). Demosthenes' selection to deliver this somber speech shows his political influence in Athens, despite the fact that his anti-Macedonian policy had resulted in the total defeat of the Greeks.

---

[4] Lyc. 1.16; [Dem.] 26.11; [Plut.], *Moralia* 849a.

[5] Aes. 3.159, 259; Dem. 18.248.

[6] "For when he heard that Philip intended to invade our land after the Battle of Chaeronea he appointed himself an envoy so that he might escape from the city. He snatched up eight talents from the treasury and left, paying no attention to the current lack of funds, when everyone else was contributing his own resources for your safety. . . . Is it right when danger threatens to entrust the city to this man, who, when he had to fight with the others against the enemy, deserted the ranks and went home, and, when he needed to be home to face danger with the others, proposed himself as an envoy and fled from the city?"

[7] On the confederacy, see Cargill 1981.

[8] Diodorus Siculus 18.56.6–7; Plut., *Alexander* 28.1–2; Pausanias 1.25.3, 34.1.

[9] On the date, see the Introduction to the *Funeral Oration*.

Moreover, his selection is also significant for the Athenians' attitude at this time to Philip: they had granted citizenship to Philip and Alexander after Chaeronea, but this move was simply a political measure arising out of a sense of relief.

Philip was now master of Greece. In the winter of 338/7, he summoned deputations from the Greek states to meet at Corinth (all but the Spartans attended), where he announced a Common Peace, headed by himself, with each state swearing an oath of loyalty to Philip and his descendants.[10] The Macedonian hegemony of Greece was thus formalized in what is commonly called the League of Corinth. A second meeting was soon held, at which Philip presented a proposal for the invasion of Persia, a variation on the panhellenic plan as put forward by Isocrates in his *To Philip* (5) of 346 (Diodorus Siculus 16.89.2).[11]

Philip never invaded Persia, for in July 336 he was assassinated at Aegae (Diodorus Siculus 16.93–95; Arrian 1.1.1). Greece immediately revolted from the Macedonian hegemony, and in Athens Demosthenes apparently dressed in festal clothes and rejoiced, even though his tenor eleven-year-old daughter had died less than a week earlier.[12] However, the new king, Alexander III (the Great), took only a few months to subdue the Greeks, reimpose the League of Corinth (Sparta again remained aloof), and prepare to invade Persia.[13]

The invasion was put on hold, for in 335 the Thebans revolted. They were supported by some states (including initially Athens; cf. Diodorus Siculus 17.8.6) and by money from the Persian king. Alexander forced Thebes to surrender, and then razed the city to the ground, in the process killing 6,000 Thebans and taking 30,000 prisoner.[14] The Athenians sent an embassy to the king stressing their loyalty and support. In reply, Alexander demanded the surrender of several leading

---

[10] Diodorus Siculus 16.89.1–3; Justin 9.5.1–6; cf. [Dem.] 17.1. See further Hammond and Griffith 1979, pp. 623–646, and Roebuck 1948.

[11] For a translation of Isoc. 5, see *Isocrates II* in this series.

[12] Aes. 3.77; Plut., *Demosthenes* 22.2; [Plut.], *Moralia* 847b.

[13] Aes. 3.161; Diodorus Siculus 17.3–4, 4.9; Arrian 1.1.1–3. On the background, see Bosworth 1988, pp. 28–33; Worthington 2004a, pp. 50–52.

[14] Diodorus Siculus 17.8.3–14.1; Arrian 1.7.1–8.8; Plut., *Demosthenes* 23.1; Justin 11.3.8. See further Hammond and Walbank 1988, pp. 56–66, and Worthington 2003a, pp. 65–86.

orators, including Demosthenes and Lycurgus, but later he relented thanks to the diplomatic intervention of Demades.[15]

Finally, in 334, Alexander left for Persia. Until his death in 323, Greece remained passive, apart from the abortive war of Agis III of Sparta in 331 to 330. He tried without success to unite the Greeks against Macedonia, and was defeated and killed by Antipater within a year (Din. 1.34; Diodorus Siculus 17.63.1–3; Curtius 6.1).[16]

Despite the cost to Greek autonomy, the Macedonian hegemony of Greece brought with it a period of peace, which allowed the Greeks some prosperity after their many decades of fighting. Nowhere was this prosperity more evident than in Athens, thanks to the administration of Lycurgus, the treasurer of the Theoric Fund, who from 336 to about 324 held power either in his own name or through subordinates.[17] Lycurgus was able to initiate a building program (this was the period when the Panathenaic Stadium and the Theatre of Dionysus were built); prepare the first official texts of the tragedies of Aeschylus, Sophocles, and Euripides (and have statues cast of them); and make other reforms, all in keeping with a new and grander era in Athenian history after the darkness of recent decades.

Then in late 324 Lycurgus was indicted, perhaps for corruption. He was carried into court on his deathbed ([Plut.] *Moralia* 842e) but successfully defended himself. After his death, his children were indicted for their father's crimes and imprisoned. They were released thanks to the letter (3) that Demosthenes wrote on their behalf while in exile.

That exile was a result of what is called the Harpalus affair of 324/3.[18] In 324, as Alexander returned to the west, his corrupt trea-

---

[15] Diodorus Siculus 17.115; Arrian 1.10.4–6; Plut., *Demosthenes* 23.4, *Phocion* 17.2; [Plut.], *Moralia* 841e, 847c, 848e.

[16] See Worthington 2004a, pp. 143–144, 150–151, and Badian 1994, pp. 258–292.

[17] Diodorus Siculus 16.88.1; [Plut.], *Moralia* 841b–844a. On Lycurgus, see further Mitchel 1970; Bosworth 1988, pp. 204–215; and the Introduction to Lycurgus in *Dinarchus, Hyperides, and Lycurgus* in this series. On the Theoric Fund, see *Letter* 3.2n50.

[18] On the Harpalus affair and its background, see in detail Worthington 1992, pp. 41–77, and Blackwell 1998. On it and its implications for Macedonia's con-

surer Harpalus fled to Greece with a force of six thousand mercenaries, five thousand talents of stolen money, and thirty warships, and sought asylum in Athens (Diodorus Siculus 17.108.6; Curtius 10.2.1). His aim was to incite the Athenians to lead the Greeks in a revolt against Macedonian power. In the meantime, Alexander's royal messenger, Nicanor, arrived in Greece with his king's Exiles Decree, to be proclaimed at the Olympic festival. The decree ordered all Greek cities (excluding Thebes) to receive back their exiles and gave Antipater the right to coerce any city that refused (Diodorus Siculus 18.8.4).[19] At the same time, there was debate among the Greeks as to whether Alexander should be worshiped as a god, although many states, including Athens, resisted this.[20]

The Exiles Decree flouted the autonomy of the Greek *poleis* since the return of exiles was outlawed under the League of Corinth's terms ([Dem.] 17.16). We might therefore expect that the Athenians would welcome Harpalus' offer of money and manpower and so revolt against Alexander, but, thanks to Demosthenes, Philocles the general was ordered to deny Harpalus entry ([Plut.], *Moralia* 846a). He went to the mercenary base at Taenarum in the southern Peloponnese, but not long after returned to Athens, this time exploiting his honorary citizen status by appealing for asylum. Philocles allowed him to enter Athens. A second Assembly meeting was held, at which Hyperides spoke in favor of accepting Harpalus' offer of support, but again Demosthenes won the day. Harpalus was imprisoned, and the money he had brought with him, allegedly seven hundred talents (Hyp. 5.9–10; cf. [Plut.], *Moralia* 846b), was impounded on the Acropolis (Din. 1.70, 89; [Plut.], *Moralia* 846b; cf. Hyp. 5.9–10), and a guard posted over it (cf. Din. 1.62). Since the Greek states were each about to send

---

trol of Greece, see Worthington 1994a, pp. 307–330. See too Faraguna 2003, esp. pp. 118–130.

[19] On the decree, see Hyp. 5.18; Diodorus Siculus 17.109.1, 18.8.2–7; Curtius 10.2.4–7; [Plut.], *Moralia* 221a; Justin 13.5.2–6; with Badian 1961, pp. 25–31, and Bosworth 1988, pp. 220–228. The Athenians would have had to return Samos, won by Timotheus over three decades earlier (see *Erotic Essay* 46n).

[20] Athenaeus 12.538b; cf. Hyp. 5.18–19; Diodorus Siculus 18.8.7; Curtius 10.2.5–7; Justin 13.5.1–6; Polybius 12.12b3; [Plut.], *Moralia* 804b, 842d; Aelian, *Varia Historia* 5.12. On Alexander's divinity, see Worthington 2004a, pp. 273–283.

an embassy to Alexander over the Exiles Decree, Demosthenes realized that harboring Harpalus would jeopardize a successful outcome for the Athenian embassy, hence his course of action.[21]

With Harpalus in prison, Demosthenes went to Olympia as head of the Athenian religious delegation—an excuse to meet with Nicanor about the Exiles Decree (Din. 1.81–82; Hyp. 5.18–19). Soon after he returned, he spoke in favor of recognizing Alexander's divine status. Although there is the insinuation in the two prosecution speeches in his later trial that he was bribed to do so (Din. 1.94, 103; Hyp. 5.31–32), it is more likely that his sudden change was intended to improve the success of the Athenian embassy to Alexander.[22]

Then things began to go wrong for Demosthenes. Soon after his imprisonment, Harpalus escaped (Diodorus Siculus 17.108.7); the people turned on Demosthenes and accused him and several others of taking bribes from Harpalus (Diodorus Siculus 17.108.8). When only half of the alleged seven hundred talents could be found, the accusations appeared valid.[23] Demosthenes proposed that the Areopagus conduct an investigation into the affair (Din. 1.1).[24] He also offered to submit to the death penalty if the Areopagus found him guilty, as did others including Philocles (Din. 3.2, 5, 16, 21; cf. Hyp. 5.34). Clearly this measure had little effect, for as the inquiry progressed, Demosthenes issued a challenge (*proklēsis*) to the people to present the Areopagus with evidence for their accusation (Din. 1.6; Hyp. 5.2). Until now, Demosthenes had protested his innocence; then he confessed he did take money not as a bribe but for the Theoric Fund (Hyp. 5.12–13).[25]

---

[21] For Demosthenes' career in this period, see Worthington 2000, pp. 90–113.

[22] That Demosthenes did not believe in Alexander's superhuman status is shown by his comment that if Alexander wanted to call himself the son of Zeus and Poseidon, so be it (Hyp. 5.31: "[Demosthenes] in the Assembly conceded that Alexander could be the son of Zeus and of Poseidon if he wanted. . . .").

[23] However, Harpalus probably lied about the figure and had with him about 450 talents: see Worthington 1992, pp. 65–69.

[24] Under this procedure, the Areopagus held an enquiry (*zētēsis*) and delivered a preliminary report (*apophasis*). If the Areopagus accused someone in its *apophasis,* that person was then put on trial and judged by a jury of his peers; see Wallace 1989, pp. 198–201.

[25] On the Theoric Fund, see *Letter* 3.2n50.

It took six months for the Areopagus to issue its report (Din. 1.45) in which it accused Demosthenes and several others of receiving bribes from Harpalus (in Demosthenes' case twenty talents of gold). Significantly, however, and something that Demosthenes would stress in his *Letters* (2.1, 15 and 3.42), it cited no evidence.[26] Around the same time, news arrived that Alexander had rejected the Athenian embassy's pleas concerning the Exiles Decree. The timing was hardly a coincidence, for Demosthenes had said that he had been sacrificed as part of a conspiracy by the Areopagus to please Alexander (*Letter* 2.2; cf. Hyp. 5.14). Demosthenes was put on trial, with several others, in about March 323.[27]

He was prosecuted by ten men, but we have only the prosecution speeches written by Dinarchus and Hyperides, as well as those written by Dinarchus against Aristogeiton and Philocles from their trials.[28] Demosthenes was condemned, as were Demades (Din. 2.15) and Philocles (*Letter* 3.31). However, the others were exculpated. After about a week's imprisonment following his trial, Demosthenes fled into exile,[29] from where he wrote several letters to the Athenians protesting his innocence in the Harpalus affair.[30]

The news that Alexander had so unexpectedly died on June 10 or 11, 323, was greeted with skepticism at first: "If Alexander were really dead, the whole world would smell from his corpse," said Demades (Plut., *Phocion* 22.3). When that death was confirmed, and with there being no

---

[26] A flaw that can even be found in the prosecution speeches at the Harpalus trials (Din. 2.21; Hyp. 5.6).

[27] Others who were tried included Aristogeiton, Aristonicus, Cephisophon, Charicles (the son-in-law of the general Phocion), Demades, Hagnonides, the general Philocles, and Polyeuctus of Sphettus; on these, see Worthington 1992, pp. 54–55.

[28] These speeches are translated in *Dinarchus, Hyperides, and Lycurgus* in this series. See further Worthington 1999, for Dinarchus' and Hyperides' speeches against Demosthenes, and Whitehead 2000, for Hyperides' speech against Demosthenes.

[29] He makes it clear in *Letter* 2.17 that he fled out of feelings of disgrace and because his advanced age would not let him cope with the hardships of being in prison.

[30] Cf. *Letter* 2.2, 14–16, 21, 26; *Letter* 3.37–38 and 43.

undisputed heir to the Macedonian throne, the Athenians were instrumental in encouraging the Greeks to revolt from Macedonia. This revolt is commonly called the Lamian War,[31] and Demosthenes saw it as his chance to return to Athens.

The Lamian War was short-lived, although a Macedonian victory was not always assured. At the strategic town of Thermopylae, the Greeks defeated the Macedonians in battle, and Antipater managed to escape to the town of Lamia for refuge. There he remained for the winter of 323/2.[32] During this time, Demosthenes had first toured the Peloponnese, and some time later, on the motion of his cousin Demon, he was officially recalled to Athens (Plut., *Demosthenes* 27). It was probably about this time that he wrote the sixth letter, urging resistance to Macedonia.

The Battle of Thermopylae was the high point for the Greeks in the Lamian War. At some point during that winter, the Athenian general Leosthenes was killed while attempting to breach Lamia (Diodorus Siculus 18.13.5; Justin 13.5.12). He was succeeded by Antiphilus, but in early spring, Antipater escaped thanks to the timely arrival of Leonnatus and 20,000 reinforcements (Diodorus Siculus 18.14.5). Although Antiphilus killed Leonnatus in battle, Antipater's escape was the break that Macedonia needed. In the summer of 322 the Greek fleet was defeated, as were the Greek land forces by Antipater at Crannon (central Thessaly). Seeing the writing on the wall, Demosthenes and Hyperides fled from Athens, and to prevent his capture, Demosthenes committed suicide by drinking poison.[33]

THE *EROTIC ESSAY* AND THE *PROLOGUES*

The *Erotic Essay* is an epideictic work, written for a youth named Epicrates, about whom nothing is known. It is influenced by both Plato and Isocrates, and echoes of their writings and beliefs are evident

---

[31] On the historical background, see Hammond and Walbank 1988, pp. 107–117; Worthington 1999, pp. 12–16; and see too Bosworth 2003.

[32] Hyp. 6.12; Diodorus Siculus 18.12.4–13.5; Plut., *Demosthenes* 27.1, *Phocion* 23.4–5; Polyaenus 4.4.2.

[33] Plut., *Demosthenes* 29.7; [Plut.], *Moralia* 847b; [Lucian], *Encomium on Demosthenes* 28, 43–49.

in it. The author attempts to counsel Epicrates and the audience on what is best for a person, the answer being the study of philosophy. Through a study of that discipline a person will become virtuous and a morally upright citizen. The content and style of the *Erotic Essay* is the most removed from Demosthenes' other writings, and it is almost certainly spurious. Based on internal evidence, it was written probably between the late 350s and 335 (so during Demosthenes' lifetime), but its author is unknown.

The *Prologues* are openings to political speeches that may well have been delivered in the Assembly. In addition to the rhetorical functions (capturing the goodwill of the audience and balancing the epilogue), these prologues give us insights into the Athenians' attitude to their democracy as well as to the audience's reactions and even expectations at an Assembly. The authorship of the prologues is disputed, but they are most likely Demosthenic, and some of them correspond closely (even at times exactly) to the prologues of his extant political speeches.[34]

NOTE ON THE TEXT

The text used in this volume is that of N. W. and N. J. DeWitt, *Demosthenes 7*, Loeb Classical Library (London: 1949; repr. 1986). Major variations between that text and others that affect the translation are cited where relevant. Other texts are:

W. Rennie, *Demosthenis Orationes,* vol. 3, Oxford Classical Text (Oxford: 1931).

R. Clavaud, *Démosthène, Discours d'apparat (Épitaphios, Éroticos),* Budé Text (Paris: 1974).

R. Clavaud, *Démosthène, Prologues,* Budé Text (Paris: 1974).

R. Clavaud, *Démosthène, Lettres et Fragments,* Budé Text (Paris: 1987).

The only commentary on any of the works in this volume is that of J. A. Goldstein, *The Letters of Demosthenes* (New York: 1968).

References in my introductions and notes to the works by author's name and text (e.g., Clavaud in the Budé Text) refer to the above.

---

[34] On authenticity, see further Worthington 2004b.

DEMOSTHENES, SPEECHES 60 AND 61, PROLOGUES, LETTERS

Translated by Ian Worthington

60. FUNERAL ORATION

INTRODUCTION

Demosthenes was chosen by the Athenians to deliver the *Funeral Oration* (*epitaphios*) over those Athenians who had died fighting Philip II of Macedonia at the Battle of Chaeronea in September 338 (Dem. 18.285, Plut., *Demosthenes* 21.2). Athens was the only *polis* in Greece to honor those who had recently died in battle with a public oration (Dem. 20.141), and this solemn ceremony, attended by foreigners as well as citizens, followed a rigid procedure. Although our principal source is the later fifth-century historian Thucydides (2.34), there is no reason to think that the procedure as he described it had changed by the later fourth century. Thucydides tells us,

> The bones of the departed lie in state for the space of three days in a tent erected for that purpose, and each one brings to his own dead any offering he desires. On the day of the funeral, coffins of cypress wood are borne on wagons, one for each tribe, and the bones of each are in the coffin of his tribe. One empty bier, covered with a pall, is carried in the procession for the missing whose bodies could not be found for burial. Anyone who wishes, whether citizen or stranger, may take part in the funeral procession, and the women who are related to the deceased are present at the burial and make lamentation. The coffins are laid in the public sepulchre, which is situated in the most beautiful suburb of the city; there they always bury those fallen in war, except indeed those who fell at Marathon; for their valor the Athenians judged to be preeminent and they buried them on the spot where they fell. But when the remains have been laid away in the earth, a man chosen by the state, who is

regarded as best endowed with wisdom and is foremost in public esteem, delivers over them an appropriate eulogy. After this the people depart.

A funeral oration belonged to the genre of epideictic (demonstrative) oratory. It dealt with honor and exhortation rather than expediency, as in the case of deliberative oratory, or justice, as in the case of forensic oratory.[1] The aim was twofold. Firstly, it was to honor those who had died with the argument that in fighting to preserve freedom (*eleutheria*) and autonomy, their deaths had not been needless. Freedom and autonomy were ideals that the Greeks valued the most and which were inherent to their *polis* system. Secondly, it was to awaken admiration in the listeners by glorifying the city, its form of government, and the exploits of its ancestors. The epideictic genre was highly rhetorical. It had a conventional or solemn formula (see further below); historical narrative within it was naturally patriotic, with the speaker lauding the deeds of the Athenians' ancestors and then linking these to praise of the more recent dead, the subject of the funeral speech.

Given the many decades in the fifth and fourth centuries that Athens was at war with other Greek states and then with Macedonia, there must have been a large number of funeral orations delivered, yet only six have survived. In chronological order, these are:

(1) Pericles' *Funeral Oration,* delivered in 430 at the end of the first year of the Peloponnesian War. Thucydides gives us a version of the speech (2.35–46), which is almost certainly not a verbatim account.

(2) Gorgias' *Funeral Oration,* of which only a fragment survives. This was probably written as a rhetorical exercise, not for delivery at an actual funeral ceremony.

(3) Lysias 2, set in the context of the Corinthian War (395–386), and perhaps dating to 392. If the speech was actually spoken and was not merely a rhetorical exercise, it must have been written for someone else, for Lysias was a metic (resident alien) and could not have delivered it himself.[2]

---

[1] On the genre, see Kennedy 1963 pp. 152–173; Loraux 1986; Usher 1999, pp. 349–352; Carey 2006; and Roisman 2006. There is an excellent discussion also by Clavaud in the Budé Text of Dem. 60.

[2] A translation of this speech by Stephen Todd is in *Lysias* in this series.

(4) Socrates' *Funeral Oration,* in Plato, *Menexenus* 236d–249c (dating to after 386). In the dialogue Socrates ascribes the speech to Aspasia of Miletus, but the references in it to the Peace of Antalcidas of 386 indicate that it cannot be by Socrates, who was executed by the Athenians in 399. It may well be the work of Plato, and if we can believe Cicero (*Orator* 151), it was read out in public annually in Athens.

(5) Demosthenes 60 (translated below).

(6) Hyperides 6, delivered by Hyperides himself at the end of the first year of the Lamian War in 322. Only part of the speech survives.[3]

All of these funeral speeches have a similarity in content and structure, and may be said to conform to a conventional structure.[4] The speaker usually begins with an apology for what he was about to say, and discusses events as far back as mythological times. The introduction (*prooimion*) is not meant to gain the goodwill of the audience but is meant to be sensational and capture attention, allowing the speaker to connect the ancestors' glorious exploits with those of the recently deceased, and to link their deaths to the defense of the common freedom (*eleutheria*) of the Greeks. Other common elements include praise of Athens and of its democracy, but the thrust of the speech is to recall the glorious exploits of the men of the past. Historical allusions are often made to the Greeks' defeat of the Persian threat to their freedom in the fifth century, especially the battles of Marathon in 490 and Salamis in 480, but it is not uncommon to find reference to the Trojan War. Then the speaker describes how, following the example set by their ancestors' exploits, the recently deceased have won immortal glory, their families are held in the highest esteem, their children will be reared by the state, and they themselves sit as heroes with the gods. The speaker may end by offering some words of condolence and even advice, often to the surviving children, and then simply dismissing his audience.

Demosthenes' speech is divided into six parts. He begins with a brief personal introduction about the importance of funeral speeches and the difficulties that face those who deliver them (1–3). This is

---

[3] A translation of this speech is in *Dinarchus, Hyperides, and Lycurgus* in this series. For a text, translation, and commentary, see Worthington 1999).

[4] For further details, see Worthington 1999, pp. 34–35.

followed by an account of the exploits of the ancestors of those who died, from the mythical era to the Persian Wars (4–14). He then moves to the present and the war against Philip II and the Battle of Chaeronea (15–26). Scattered throughout this part is praise of the nature and patriotic spirit of those who died. An excursus follows on the ten Athenian tribes and their origins (27–31), before another eulogy to those who died and are now in paradise (32–34). The speech ends with the customary consolation to the families of the deceased (35–37) and dismissal (37).

An exact date for the speech cannot be determined. We might expect the speaker to refer to Philip's dealings with the other Greek states after the Battle of Chaeronea and especially the establishment of the League of Corinth. However, the League is not mentioned, and the only peace to which the speaker refers is that between Philip and Athens after the battle (60.20). The tone of the speech with its references to the Greeks' mere "present misfortunes" seems to indicate a date prior to the formation of the League, for present misfortunes are very different from Macedonian hegemony and the end of Greek autonomy. Since Chaeronea was fought on September 1, we must allow time for Philip's peace terms to be communicated to the Athenians and accepted by them, and especially for Demosthenes' return from his grain commission.[5] A date sometime in late 338 would be the most plausible.[6]

The authenticity of the speech is disputed. In antiquity it was regarded as spurious, and a majority of modern scholars follow suit.[7] However, there are indications in the speech that it is Demosthenic (see notes to sections 18, 19, 31), and in his *On the Crown* of 330 there are echoes of his use of fate and the gods' role (e.g., 18.194, 207–208, 253–255, 303, 306). Indeed, in the appeals to freedom, the reputation of Athens, and the role of fortune there is much that is in keeping with an *epitaphios*. One argument that this speech is spurious is the catalogue of the ten Athenian tribes (27–31), which seems out of place. Yet we should not forget that departures from any norm were known; for example, Hyperides' eulogy to the Athenian general Leosthenes in his

---

[5] On the historical background, see the Introduction.

[6] Cf. Clavaud in the Budé Text, p. 11: "4 Novembre (?)."

[7] E.g., Blass 1898, pp. 356–358; Dobson 1919, p. 267.

funeral oration.[8] Demosthenes may well have seized the opportunity afforded by this occasion to do something remarkable. Moreover, the speech's nature meant that its style should be different, just as the funeral orations of Lysias (2) or of Hyperides (6) are quite different from their forensic speeches.

While the speech may not be on a par with Demosthenes' other speeches,[9] we should not forget how hard a task it must have been for him to write against the background of his failed anti-Macedonian policy. For the moment, the matter of its authenticity cannot be absolutely determined, but we should not immediately reject what we have just because it is different from Demosthenes' other speeches, and I have argued elsewhere that it is genuine.[10]

60. FUNERAL ORATION

[1] When the city decreed to hold a public funeral for those who lie in this tomb[11] because they proved brave in the war, and it appointed me to give the customary eulogy for them, I at once began to think how they might receive fitting praise. However, while studying and thinking about this, I discovered that to speak properly about the dead was an impossible task.[12] Since they scorned the passion for life, which is inherent in everyone, preferring to die nobly than live and see Greece suffer misfortune, how can the example of courage left behind not surpass the power of any speech? Nevertheless, I have decided to address the subject in the same way as those who, on previous occasions, have spoken in this place.

[2] That the city pays serious attention to those who die in battle is especially evident from (among other things) this law by which it selects

---

[8] See Worthington 1999, pp. 35–36.

[9] Cf. Loraux 1986, pp. 254–255; Clavaud in the Budé Text, pp. 20–25.

[10] See Worthington 2003c, pp. 152–157.

[11] The public tomb was situated in the district of Athens known as the Ceramicus, taking its name from the potters and painters who lived and worked there from the sixth century onwards.

[12] This type of opening is common to funeral orations, where the speaker hopes to offset any criticism he might face for his speech by admitting the Herculean labor that he faces.

the speaker at the public funerals. For knowing that noble men spurn the acquisition of wealth and the enjoyment of the material pleasures of life, and direct all their efforts toward virtue and praise, the people thought that they should be honored with speeches, which best ensured that they would receive these, so that the glory they had won in life would also be granted to them in death. [3] Therefore, if I found that among the qualities that lead to virtue, courage alone was theirs, I would just praise this and stop talking; but since it was their lot to have been nobly born and rigorously educated to acquire wisdom, and to have dedicated their lives to the highest goals, which would properly confirm their excellence, I would be ashamed if I were seen to omit any of these points. So I will begin with the origin of their heritage.

[4] From the dawn of time, everyone has acknowledged the nobility of these men's birth. For they and each of their ancestors before them can trace their heritage not only to a human father but also to this entire land, which they all share in common and in which they are recognized as indigenous.[13] For they alone of all people lived in this land from which they were born and handed it on to their descendants. Thus, it would be right to think that those who arrive in cities as migrants and are called citizens of these cities are like adopted children but that these men are legitimate citizens of their land by birth.[14] [5] I also think the fact that the fruits of the earth, by which people live, appeared first among us,[15] apart from being the greatest service to all humankind, is an acknowledged sign that our land is the mother of our ancestors. For all creatures that bear young by their very nature

---

[13] The speaker refers to the Athenians' belief that, as with Cecrops cited in 30, they were born of the land itself (autochthonous), an ideal prevalent in all types of oratory; cf. Thuc. 2.36; Lys. 2.47; Plato, *Menexenus* 237b – c; Hyp. 6.7 (funeral); Dem. 18.205 (forensic). The belief underpins the Athenians' feelings of superiority over other Greeks, as the speaker goes on to say.

[14] For the same idea, see Hyp. 6.7.

[15] A reference to olives, which Athens claimed as its own special crop. A myth told of the contest between Athena and Poseidon for possession of Athens; Athena was victorious when she created an olive tree and thus became Athens' patron deity. Grain is said to have been introduced by the grain goddess Demeter at Eleusis (a village that was part of Attica).

at the same time provide nourishment for their offspring, which is exactly what our land has done.

[6] Therefore, such are the attributes of good birth, which these men's ancestors have possessed throughout time. However, I shrink from mentioning everything to do with courage and their other virtues to make sure my speech does not become too long for the occasion. But those exploits that are useful to recall to those who already know them, and also best for those who do not hear, deeds which inspire great admiration and do not require a long tiresome speech, these I will attempt to talk about briefly. [7] For the ancestors of the present generation, both their fathers and those before them who had names by which they are recognized by members of their family,[16] never wronged any person, Greek or barbarian. Instead, in addition to all their other fine qualities, they were most just, and they performed many gallant deeds in their own defense.[17] [8] They defeated the invading army of Amazons so thoroughly that it fled beyond the Phasis river,[18] and they drove the army of Eumolpus and his many allies not only out of their land but also from the rest of Greece, although all those who lived in front of us to the West could not withstand them or turn them back.[19] What is more, they were called the saviors of the

---

[16] After the democratic reforms of Cleisthenes in 508, an Athenian citizen identified himself by his own name, that of his father (patronymic) and the deme where he lived (demotic), a style that remained the norm throughout Athenian history. Names tended to be repeated within families; an especially common practice was to name a boy after his grandfather. See 27 for another aspect of Cleisthenes' legislation, and on his work see, e.g., Forrest 1966, pp. 190–203.

[17] The following are stock examples: see Lys. 2.4–16; Isoc. 4.55–58, 68–70; Plato, *Menexenus* 239a.

[18] The Amazons were fierce female warriors who lived on the boundaries of the known world. They appear in the *Iliad* (3.189, 6.186), and another early epic recorded how Achilles killed their queen. According to legend (Plut., *Theseus* 26–27), they sought revenge on the fabled Athenian king Theseus, perhaps for his support of Heracles in his labor of stealing the girdle of their queen Hippolyte, and besieged him in Athens. This war lasted for three months before Theseus concluded a treaty with them. The Phasis river is in Colchis in northern Greece. On Theseus, cf. 28.

[19] Eumolpus, a son of Poseidon, invaded Greece from Thrace, and came as far as Eleusis, where Erechtheus killed him in battle (cf. 27).

sons of Heracles, who himself saved others, when they were fleeing from Eurystheus and came to this land as suppliants.[20] And in addition to all these and many other fine deeds, they did not allow the established rites of the departed to be insulted when Creon forbade the burial of the seven against Thebes.[21]

[9] I have ignored many (other) deeds which are regarded as myths, and have recalled only those events which have each been the subject of so many honorable stories that the poets who compose in regular meters or in song,[22] and many of those who write treatises, have made their deeds the subject of their own compositions. But I will now mention achievements which are no less deserving of glory than those but are closer to us in time and so have not yet become household stories or been raised to heroic stature. [10] Our ancestors alone twice repelled by land and by sea the horde which invaded from the whole of Asia,[23] and through their own individual risk were responsible for securing the common safety of all Greeks. And although what I intend to say next has been said by others before me, this should not prevent those men from receiving their rightful and just praise. It would be reasonable to consider them better than those who waged war against Troy, for the latter were the best men from all Greece, but

---

[20] The Dorian Greeks claimed a connection with Heracles and attributed the seizure of the Peloponnese to his sons. At first they were repelled by Eurystheus (Hyllus, Heracles' eldest son, was killed), but eventually they were successful.

[21] When Creon, king of Thebes, refused to allow the burial of fallen Argive heroes who had attacked Thebes, Theseus gave help to their suppliant wives (see Euripides' *Suppliants*).

[22] Poets used regular meters for epic poems and plays, which were recited. They used song for odes and dithyrambs (choral odes), which were sung to music.

[23] The reference to the Persian Wars of 490–479 is one of the most frequent *topoi* in Greek oratory. In 490, the Persian King Darius sent an army to Greece. It landed at Marathon in eastern Attica but was defeated by the Athenians and Plataeans. In 481, the Persians under Xerxes again invaded Greece. They defeated a Spartan army at Thermopylae in 480, but in the same year their navy was resoundingly defeated at Salamis, and Xerxes fled back to Persia. The following year the remnants of the Persian army were defeated in battle at Plataea. On the same day, according to Herodotus (9.90), what was left of the Persian fleet was defeated at Mycale in Ionia. See further Herod. 6–9; Burn 1984; and Green 1996.

they captured only one place in Asia with great difficulty after be-
sieging it for ten years,[24] [11] whereas the former not only repelled the
horde that invaded from a whole continent, which had already subjected every other country, but also imposed punishment for the
wrongs done to the other Greeks. Moreover, they prevented acts of
self-aggression among the Greeks themselves, and faced any danger
that happened to arise, and aligned themselves on whichever side justice assigned them, until time leads us to the generation alive today.

[12] Let no one think I listed these achievements because I do not
know what I should say about each of them. For if I was the least skillful of all men at indicating what must be said, the very valor of those
men shows deeds that are available and are easy to relate. However, I
prefer to recall their noble birth and the great deeds performed by their
ancestors, and then to connect my account as quickly as possible to the
deeds of these men, in order that, just as they were kinsmen by nature,
I might praise both of them together. I assume this would be pleasing
to them, and especially to both groups, if they should share in each
other's valor not only by their birth but also in my words of praise.

[13] In the meantime, I must pause and, before presenting the
deeds of these men, appeal to the goodwill of those who followed us
to the burial, although not of our people.[25] For if I had been commis-
sioned to honor this burial with an expenditure of money or by an
equestrian or gymnastic spectacle, then the more eagerly and more
lavishly I would have organized these, the more I would have been
thought to have done what was appropriate. But since I was appointed
to praise these men in a speech, I am afraid that, without the sympathy of my audience, in my enthusiasm I may have just the opposite
effect. [14] For wealth and speed and strength, and all other such qualities, are advantageous for their possessors by themselves, and whoever
happens to have them wins in those areas, even if no one else wants
them to. But to be persuasive a person's words require the goodwill of

---

[24] The Trojan War was a patriotic *topos,* as was the view that it was less important than the Persian Wars. Note the similarity in wording to Isoc. 4.83, as we
would expect in the employment of a popular *topos.*

[25] This probably refers to the metics (noncitizen residents of Athens) and other
foreigners, who also attended state funeral ceremonies (Thuc. 2.34.4; cf. 2.36.4).

his audience. With its goodwill, even a speech of average quality brings glory and gains favor, but without it, even an extremely fine speaker offends his listeners.

[15] Now, I could cite many exploits for which these men would rightly be praised, but when I consider their deeds I am at a loss what to mention first. For they all come into my head at the same time, making the choice among them difficult. Nevertheless, I will try to put my speech in the same order as the course of these men's lives. [16] From the beginning, these men excelled in all aspects of their upbringing; at each stage of life, they had the appropriate training, and they pleased all those whom they should have—parents, friends, relatives. For that reason, the thoughts of their relatives and friends now longingly recall these men at any hour, and like seeing familiar footprints those now alive seize upon the many reminders they recognized of their excellence. [17] And when they arrived at manhood, they made their character known not only to their fellow citizens but also to all people. For the beginning of all virtue is wisdom—indeed it is—and the end is courage: with the one a person understands what should be done; with the other he carries it out. These men excelled by far in both. [18] For if any danger threatened all the Greeks in common, these men were first to recognize it, and so often they exhorted everyone to save the situation, which is an illustration of purpose and right thinking.[26] And when the Greeks manifested slackness, mixed with folly, and did not anticipate some dangers and feigned ignorance of others, although these could have been safely prevented, nevertheless, when they did listen and wanted to do what was necessary,[27] these men did not bear malice. Coming forward and eagerly offering everything—bodies, money, and allies—they marched to the test of the battle, in which they spared nothing, not even their lives.

---

[26] Chaeronea did not ensure everyone's safety, for it was a Greek defeat. Here and in the next sentence, the speaker is referring to the Athenians' reluctance to confront the danger from Philip immediately and to the warfare that resulted. Similar phraseology is found in Dem. 18.19–20, 62 (cf. 159), which refers to Demosthenes' own career and his exhortation of the people to recognize and combat the danger from Philip. The parallel helps to support the case for the speech's authenticity.

[27] Reference to the Athenians' alliance with Thebes in 339 against Philip that led to the Battle of Chaeronea.

[**19**] Whenever a battle takes place, one side must win and the other must lose. However, I would not hesitate to say that I think that those who die at their posts on either side do not share in defeat but are equally victorious on both sides. For among the living victory is decided by divine dispensation, but every man who stands firm in battle has done what he ought to do to achieve this end. But if—being only human—he meets his destiny, his misfortune is due to chance,[28] but his opponents did not defeat his spirit. [**20**] In my view, the reason why our land was not invaded by the enemy, besides their own poor judgment, was the courage of these men. For those who engaged them there in that battle got proof of their valor man by man, and did not wish to face the relatives of those men in battle once again; they would be facing men of the same mettle, but they suspected that they would not so easily gain the help of chance.[29]

This is clear especially from the peace that was made. For you cannot cite a more true or more honorable reason for this than that the enemy commander[30] admired the courage of those who died, and wished to be friends with their relatives rather than to endanger all his achievements again. [**21**] I think that if you were to ask those on the other side if they thought their victory was due to their own courage or to an unexpected and harsh change of fortune and the experience and daring of their commander, not one would be so shameless or presumptuous as to claim credit for the result. Moreover, in cases where the divine spirit, the master of all men, decides the outcome as he wishes, all others, being human, must be acquitted of the charge of cowardice.[31] And when

---

[28] The reference to chance or Fate (*tychē*) emphasizes its role in human affairs, that responsibility for men's fate lies not with themselves but with chance; cf. 23, Hyp. 6.13. Such references to chance are almost everywhere in Greek literature. Elsewhere in his works, Demosthenes assigns this role to *tychē* in *On the Crown* (18.194, 207–208, 253–255, 303, 306), which supports the case for the present speech's authenticity.

[29] After the Battle of Chaeronea, the Athenians feared that Philip would invade Attica and besiege Athens, but instead he made peace with them. By contrast, he treated their allies harshly.

[30] Philip II.

[31] See the Introduction to this speech on the reference to cowardice perhaps pointing to a Demosthenic authorship.

the leader of our enemies overcame those in charge of our army, no one could fairly blame the rank and file of either the enemy or us. [**22**] But if there is any person who might properly be blamed for the outcome of that battle, one might reasonably accuse the Thebans in charge of their army, not the rank and file of the Thebans or us. For they took command of a force with an unconquerable spirit that never sought excuses, and an enviable love of personal glory, but made proper use of none of these.[32] [**23**] On other points, each man has an opinion and may draw his own conclusions. But it has become equally clear to all who are living that the freedom of all Greece depended on the lives of these men. At any rate, since fate bore them away, not one of those who survived has faced the enemy. My speech should be free of ill will, but it seems to me that if someone says that the courage of these men was the very soul of Greece, he speaks the truth; [**24**] for as soon as their breath left their bodies the honor of Greece was gone. Perhaps we will seem to exaggerate, still it must be said: it is as if someone removed the light from our universe, and all that remained of our life became bitter and harsh; so, because these men have been carried off, all the previous glory of Greece has fallen into darkness and infamy.[33]

[**25**] Many factors undoubtedly contributed to their character, not least of which was our constitution, which inspired them.[34] For oligarchies run by a few produce fear in their citizens, but do not foster a sense of duty. So, when the test of war comes, every man saves himself to the best of his ability, for he knows that if he wins over his masters with gifts or any other service whatsoever, no matter how shamefully he

---

[32] The criticism of the Theban command is harsh since Philip's superior tactics spelled the Greeks' doom. However, Demosthenes may be trying to remove any blame from the 300-strong Theban Sacred Band, which stood fast against the Macedonian army and was annihilated by the future Alexander III, then aged eighteen (Plut., *Alexander* 9.2; cf. Diodorus Siculus 16.86.3–4). See further Rahe 1981, pp. 84–87.

[33] Compare Pericles' "spring has been taken out of the year," quoted by Arist., *Rhetoric* 1.7, 3.10, though the words do not appear in the funeral oration in Thucydides.

[34] The superiority of democracy is a common theme in Athenian oratory; cf. Plato, *Menexenus* 239d–248b and Thuc. 2.37–43. On exploiting the Athenians' fear of oligarchy, cf. *Letter* 1.1–2; the Introduction to *Prologues;* and *Prologues* 2, 42.

has acted, only a little blame will attach to him afterwards. [26] But democracies have many noble and just qualities, to which sensible people must be loyal, and in particular freedom of speech, which cannot be prevented from showing the truth because it is based on speaking the truth. Those who do something wrong cannot possibly win over everyone; and a single man voicing the appropriate reprimand does not cause the offender pain.[35] And those who themselves would never speak a slanderous word are pleased to hear it spoken by another. All these men feared such criticisms, quite rightly, and to avoid the shame of future reprimands,[36] they stalwartly faced the danger coming from our enemies, and chose a noble death rather than a disgraceful life.

[27] I have told the general reasons why all these chose to die nobly: birth, upbringing, being accustomed to the best ways of living, and the principles of our whole constitution. I shall now tell you what inspired the men in each tribe to be brave.[37] All the Erechtheidae knew that Erechtheus, after whom they were named, gave his own daughters, who are called Hyacinthides, to certain death, and killed them in order to save this land.[38] For this reason, they considered it a disgrace if they should be seen placing greater value on their mortal bodies than on their immortal reputation when someone born from the

---

[35] I follow the Oxford Classical Text of Rennie. The speaker means that, in oligarchies, it is a simple matter for criminals to persuade those few in power, but in democracies, where the mass of the citizens have voting rights and the power to legislate, such persuasion is impossible.

[36] Cf. Pericles' *Funeral Oration* (Thuc. 2.37.3) and Hyp. 6.25 on fear of exposure in democracies, which were rooted on the rule of law (on this, cf. *Prologue* 12.2).

[37] The Attic population was originally divided into four tribes. In 508, in an effort to reduce the power of the aristocracy in the local areas, the archon Cleisthenes divided the population into ten tribes (*Ath. Pol.* 21), each composed of people from different geographical areas of Attica. He also introduced tribal Assemblies that considered matters affecting their particular tribes and elected various officials. The following list is our main source material for the ten Athenian tribes.

[38] In this Athenian version of the myth, Erechtheus, one of the kings of Athens, had three daughters (or four, depending on the tradition). When Eumolpus of Thrace invaded Attica (see 8), the Delphic oracle told Erechtheus that he would have to sacrifice one of his daughters in order to save it. This he did, and Attica was saved. The other daughters apparently took their own lives. The story forms the plot of Euripides' lost *Erechtheus*.

immortals had done everything to keep his own land. [**28**] The Aegeidae knew that Theseus, the son of Aegeus, first gave everyone in the city the right to speak.[39] They thought it terrible to betray his principles and chose to die rather than to lose them and live among the Greeks clinging passionately to life. The Pandionidae knew the story of the daughters of Pandion, Procne and Philomela, who punished Tereus for his hybris against themselves.[40] They did not think life was worth living unless they demonstrated a courage similar to their kinship with those women, when they saw the abuses inflicted on Greece.

[**29**] The Leontidae had heard the stories that told of how the daughters of Leo gave themselves as an offering to the citizens on behalf of their country,[41] and they felt it would be wrong, when those women showed such manly spirit, if they, as men, should be shown to have less. The Acamantidae remembered the epics in which Homer says that Acamas sailed to Troy for the sake of his mother Aethra.[42] So if Acamas faced every danger to save his own mother, how could these men not decide to brave every danger to save all their parents at home? [**30**] The Oeneidae were aware that Semele was the daughter of Cadmus and the mother of one whom it is not fitting to name at this

---

[39] Theseus, another of Athens' legendary kings and famous for slaying the Minotaur of King Minos of Crete, was responsible for uniting together the various districts of Attica into one state with Athens at the head, a process called *synoikismos* (Thuc. 2.15; Plut., *Theseus* 24). He is represented as a democratic hero in literature (e.g., Euripides, *Supplices* 352–353; Plut., *Theseus* 25.1–3). On Theseus, see also 8.

[40] Procne was the wife of the Thracian king Tereus, an ally of Pandion of Athens. Tereus treacherously lured her sister Philomela to his court by pretending Procne was dead. He then raped Philomela and cut off her tongue to prevent her speaking of the crime. When Procne found out, she served Tereus a meal of their child Itys, and both women escaped with the gods' help.

[41] Leo, son of Orpheus, had three daughters, Phasithea, Theope and Euboule, whom he sacrificed on the orders of the Delphic oracle in order to end a terrible famine affecting the Athenians. In gratitude, they built a shrine to the girls in the Ceramicus, the same district in which the tomb of the fallen soldiers was located and the funeral oration was held.

[42] Aethra was the mother of Theseus, and Acamas was his son, hence Aethra's grandson (not her son, as stated here). She was a handmaiden of Helen (*Iliad* 3.144), and was brought home by her grandsons after the fall of Troy.

tomb, from whom Oeneus was born, who was called the founder of their tribe.[43] Since that danger was common to both their states, they thought they should face every struggle on behalf of both. The Cecropidae knew that their founder was said to be part dragon and part man, only because he resembled a man in intelligence and a dragon in strength.[44] So they considered it their duty to undertake deeds worthy of both. [31] The Hippothoöntidae remembered the wedding of Alope, from whom Hippothoön was born, and they knew him as their founder.[45] I must observe propriety on this occasion, and so I pass over plain speech.[46] They thought that they should be seen to be carrying out exploits worthy of them. The Aeantidae were aware that after Ajax was robbed of the spoils of valor, he considered his own life unlivable.[47] Thus, when the divinity gave the spoils of bravery to another, they thought they should die while warding off the enemy and so not suffer ignominy themselves. The Antiochidae did not forget that Antiochus was the son of Heracles.[48] Therefore, they decided they should either live worthily of their heritage or die with dignity.

---

[43] This was Dionysus (Bacchus), god of wine and of harvests. It was not permissible to state the name of an Olympian god at a funeral ceremony. Semele, daughter of Cadmus of Thebes, was impregnated by Zeus and gave birth to Dionysus (she was later killed thanks to a jealous Hera). Dionysus' son Oeneus is not to be confused with the Oeneus in Homer. There were two Attic demes called Oenoë, neither of them in the tribe Oeneidae. Demosthenes treats the tribe as having loyalty to Thebes as well as Athens, the two main cities fighting against Philip at Chaeronea.

[44] Cecrops, supposedly the first king of Athens, was said to have had the upper body of a man and the lower of a serpent or dragon (cf. Euripides, *Ion* 1163–1164) and was born of the land (autochthonous).

[45] Hippothoön was the son of Poseidon and Alope; twice left to die, he was saved on both occasions and fed on the milk of a mare. This was a common custom among the Scythians (Herod. 4.2).

[46] Clavaud in the Budé Text suggests that Demosthenes was exhibiting the same scruples here as in 30, when referring to an Olympian god in a funeral oration.

[47] Ajax (Greek *Aias*) was clearly the best Greek fighter in the Trojan War after Achilles, but when Achilles died, his armor was given to Odysseus and not Ajax, who could not live with this disgrace and killed himself (*Odyssey* 11.541–567).

[48] Demosthenes seems to be grasping at straws for an eponymous hero for the Antiochidae since we know next to nothing about Antiochus, son of the Dryopian princess Meda and apparently Heracles (cf. Diodorus Siculus 4.37).

[**32**] The living relatives of these dead are to be pitied for their loss of such men and their separation from a close and intimate friendship. The affairs of our country are made desolate and full of tears and grief; however, it is fair to conclude that those who died are fortunate. First, in exchange for a short period of life,[49] they leave behind for all time an ageless glory in which their children will be raised in honor, and their parents will be maintained in old age, admired by all, and the glory of these men will console them in their grief.[50] [**33**] Next, their bodies are free of sickness and their souls know no pain, which the living have to bear as circumstances dictate,[51] and they receive the traditional rites[52] with great honor and much admiration. The whole country gives them a public burial, and they alone receive public eulogies; but their relatives and fellow citizens are not alone in mourning them, for every country which can be called Greece and the greater part of the inhabited world also join their grieving. How can we not consider them fortunate? [**34**] Someone might fairly say that these men are assistants to the gods below, and have the same position in the islands of the blessed as the brave men from earlier times. Although no eyewitness has reported this fact about them, if we can predict the future on the basis of appearance, we conclude that those whom we the living judge worthy of honor in this world will receive the same honor down there.

[**35**] It is difficult, I suppose, to lighten present misfortunes with a speech, but we must try nevertheless to turn our minds to consolation, and realize that it is a fine thing for those who gave birth to men such as these, and were themselves born of similar stock, to be seen bearing these tribulations more gracefully than others, and to remain the same no matter what fortune befalls them. [**36**] This conduct would be especially fitting and honorable for them, and would bring the greatest repute to the whole city and those who still live. It is hard for fathers

---

[49] The idea that those who die nobly gain an immortal fame goes back to Homer and is common in funeral orations (Lys. 2.79–81; Thuc. 2.43–44; Hyp. 6.24, 27).

[50] For the law making the state responsible for raising war orphans, see Aes. 3.154. References to the state's maintenance of children are common in funeral orations (Thuc. 2.44.3–4, 46.1; Plato, *Menexenus* 246d–247e, 249a; Hyp. 6.27).

[51] For the sentiment in 33–34, cf. Hyp. 6.43.

[52] Every year a sacrifice and then athletic contests were held at the public tomb in memory of the deceased.

and mothers to be robbed of their children and to be without their dearest family to care for them in their old age.[53] However, it is a majestic thing to see that they have immortal honor and a public memorial of their virtue and are thought to deserve sacrifices and games in perpetuity.[54] [37] It is painful for children to lose their father, but it is a fine thing to inherit a father's glorious reputation. We will find that this pain is brought by the divinity, to whom mortal men must yield, but that distinction and virtue result from the free choice of those who were willing to die nobly.

I did not think how I might speak at length, but how I might speak the truth. And now that you have grieved, and properly performed the customary rites, you should depart.

---

[53] By a law allegedly of Solon in 594, children were required to support their parents in old age and give them a proper burial: *Ath. Pol.* 56.6; Dem. 24.103–107 (the law is quoted at 105); Is. 1.39 and 8.32; Plut., *Solon* 22.4, with Lacey 1968, pp. 116–118. On Solon, see further *Erotic Essay* 49.

[54] On these, see 33.

61. EROTIC ESSAY

‹‹‹

INTRODUCTION

As with the *Funeral Oration,* the *Erotic Essay* is an example of epideictic or demonstrative oratory. The aim was not to persuade the audience to adopt a particular viewpoint but to exhort it and excite its
admiration.[1] This essay was not a speech as such but a rhetorical exercise, to be read out perhaps at a symposium. It takes the form of a di-
dactic discourse, much influenced by Platonic thought (see below) on
what is best for a person, that works on two levels: as a speech for the
young Epicrates and as an address to the speaker's audience. There are
many echoes of the love speech attributed to Lysias, which is contained
in Plato's *Phaedrus,* as well as of works by Isocrates, especially the *Evagoras* (Isoc. 9), which is also epideictic. Since many of these are merely
commonplaces, we would expect to find them occurring often.

In this essay, a young man, Epicrates, apparently of extraordinary
beauty, is eulogized by another (unnamed) man, perhaps his teacher,
for his looks and physical prowess, and then encouraged to study philosophy in order to improve his mind and so become virtuous. If successful, he will become a morally upright citizen, who will engage in
political life and so serve his city well. We do not know who Epicrates
was, nor even if he was a real person, although the speaker indicates
that Epicrates did turn up to hear the essay (2).

The essay is divided into six broad parts. The speaker has a brief
preamble on the nature of his work and on Epicrates, who arrives at
its end (1–2). Then the speech proper begins with an explanation of
why the speaker has written his essay, and the base and pure motives

---

[1] On the genre, see the Introduction to *Funeral Oration.*

of those attracted to physical beauty (3–9). We then have a eulogy to Epicrates: his appearance, his character, his intelligence, his physical prowess, and his courage (10–33). Sections 33 to 36 are a recapitulation of the speaker's intentions and lead into the lengthy exhortation that Epicrates must study philosophy above all other disciplines, both for his own personal virtue and to allow him to play a greater role in political life, in a section called the protrepticus (37–55).[2] The essay has a brief conclusion at 57.

The feelings that the male composer of this work expresses for the young Epicrates go beyond friendship, thus reflecting that in ancient Greek society same-sex relationships were condoned. The ancient Greek name for sexual relations between men and boys was *paiderastia* (hence, the English word pederasty), and in a male-to-male relationship the partners took on different roles: the *eromenos,* the one who was loved (passive), and the *erastes,* the one who did the loving (active; cf. 3). It was not unusual for the *eromenos* to be a mere youth and the *erastes* an adult male. The *erastes* was primarily responsible for helping the young man's moral, political, and intellectual development, and this could lead to a sexual relationship.[3]

Plato made a distinction between love that has only a physical basis (lust), and love that stems from the quality of the person loved, especially his moral qualities, in two of his works, the *Phaedrus* and *Symposium.* Thus, we have a concept of spiritual love as distinct from plain lust. The author of the *Erotic Essay* has obviously been influenced by both Isocrates and Plato, for the work falls into this "class" of sexual admiration for a young man but with the relationship anchored firmly on the youth's moral and intellectual development for his own good. There is much similarity with Plato's *Phaedrus.*[4] However, the influence seems to extend beyond the moral and philosophical, for it is probably not coincidental that it was at the house of an Epicrates that the orator Lysias was supposed to have delivered his speech on love (Plato, *Phaedrus* 227b). The speech is given in the *Phaedrus,* but it is not certain

---

[2] Protreptics were writings that aimed at persuading young men to study philosophy.

[3] See further, e.g., Dover 1978 and Halperin 1990.

[4] On the Platonic influence and thought here, see Clavaud in the Budé Text, pp. 70–77.

whether this is Lysianic or Platonic in composition. This type of *Erotic Essay* thus becomes a genre in itself, quite different from the earlier poems that professed love for those of the same sex, for example, those by Theognis or by Sappho. As such, the genre of the erotic essay enjoys a long history, for we have one in the *Moralia* attributed to Plutarch of the late first or early second century AD (748e–771e).

The *Erotic Essay* is so different in style and content from Demosthenes' other writings that it is usually regarded as spurious.[5] The essay indicates that the author was an Athenian (see 23, 25, 35, 54), but it is hard to imagine someone like Demosthenes writing this work when he was so preoccupied with first legal matters and then public affairs for all his career. The style also is very unlike that of Demosthenes; for example, it has long antithetical sentences, more in keeping with Isocrates' style, repetition of sentences, and habitual self-reflection. It may even have been written by a pupil of Isocrates.

Its date is also unknown.[6] It cannot be earlier than the fourth century, given the references to Timotheus (46), Thebes (25), and the Seven Sages (50), as well as the parallels with some of Isocrates' speeches, especially the *Antidosis* of 350. It is possible to narrow the date for the work to between 350 and 335 in view of the description of Timotheus' activities as recent (he died in the late 350s) and the present-tense allusion to Thebes (which was destroyed in 335).

61. EROTIC ESSAY

[1] Well then, since you want to hear the essay, I will bring it out and read it to you. But first, you must understand its intention.[7] The writer of the essay wants to praise Epicrates, whom he considers

---

[5] E.g., by Blass 1898, pp. 358–360, and Dobson 1919, p. 267; Clavaud in the Budé Text, pp. 85–89, accepts it as genuine. The DeWitts in the Loeb edition, p. 41, leave the matter open.

[6] Clavaud in the Budé Text, p. 85, dates it between 340 and the early months of 323.

[7] Socrates begins the love speech at Plato, *Phaedrus* 237c in much the same way, so it is probably a common opening: "One must know what the advice is about, or it is sure to be utterly futile. . . ."

the most pleasing among the many good and noble[8] young men in the city and who surpasses his contemporaries more in wisdom than in physical beauty. Seeing how, to put it bluntly, the majority of erotic compositions bring shame rather than honor to those about whom they are written, he has taken care that this not happen, and has written what he says his own judgment has convinced him, that a virtuous lover would not do anything shameful nor even demand it. [2] This is what you might take to be the most erotic part of the essay. The remainder in part praises the young man himself and in part advises him about his education and goals in life. All of it is written in a manner for someone to put into a book, for works intended for a listening audience should be written simply, much the same as someone might say something off the cuff, but those that are designed to last for a long time should be composed poetically and elaborately.[9] For the former should persuade but the latter should display the author's talent.[10] Therefore, in order that I do not tell you more than the speech does or expound on what I myself know about these topics, pay attention as you are now going to hear the speech itself—for the very person whom I wanted to hear it has come—Epicrates.

[3] Now I see that some of those who are loved (*eromenos*) and endowed with beauty make the right use of neither of these benefits, but take on grand airs because of their fine appearance and are loath to associate with their lovers (*erastes*). Far from judging what is best, because of those who ruin love relationships, they also have an ill attitude towards those whose motive for love is pure. So I decided that such men not only do themselves a disservice but also breed bad habits in others. [4] In my view, those who are sensible should not follow the folly of these men but should consider especially that, since actions are not simply honorable or disgraceful but for the most part differ according to the people involved, it is unreasonable to hold one opinion about both situations. It is the most ridiculous of all, moreover, to envy those who

---

[8] *Kalos kagathos,* a specific term that indicated the person was of noble descent and morally good.

[9] There is a reference to these two styles at Isoc. 4.11, where Isocrates says that "both kinds should be alike and should not be distinguished, the one by plainness of style, the other by display."

[10] Literally "the latter should be *epideiktikous.*"

have the greatest number and the most steadfast of friends and to reject their lovers, who are a private group and alone naturally form friendships not with everyone but with those who are beautiful and modest.

[5] And indeed, for those who have never seen such a friendship yet turn out well, or who have vehemently condemned themselves, assuming they would not be able innocently to associate with acquaintances, it is perhaps not unreasonable to think this. But for those like you, who are not completely ignorant of the many benefits that accumulate through love without shame and have lived all their life with the most careful prudence, it is unreasonable to have even a suspicion that they would do anything base. [6] Therefore, I am even more prompted to write this speech, thinking that I will not fail to achieve two of the finest objectives. First, by listing your good qualities I hope to show both that you are someone to be emulated and that I am not foolish if I desire such a person as you. Second, in advising you about what is particularly urgent, I think I will show my own goodwill and provide a foundation for our mutual friendship.

[7] However, I am aware that it is hard to do you justice in describing your nature and that it is still more dangerous to offer advice and thus make oneself liable to the person he persuades. But I consider that those who justly receive praise should exceed the ability of those who praise them by surpassing them with true virtue, and I will not err in my advice, for I know that even the best advice could not be rightly carried out by those who are foolish and completely ruined by extravagance, but that even moderately good advice cannot fail to succeed in the hands of those who choose to live wisely and blamelessly.

[8] It is with such hopes as these that I now embark on my speech. I think that everyone would agree with me that it is especially urgent for youths of this age to possess beauty in their appearance, wisdom in their souls, and courage in both of these, and to have a continuing grace in their words. Not only has Fortune so generously bestowed on you the advantages of nature that you continually excite wonder and admiration, but through your own diligence you are advancing in other respects to the point that no well-disposed person could criticize you. [9] And yet what sort of man is worthy of the greatest praise?[11]

---

[11] Cf. Isoc. 16.30: "Really, what is required of the man who is thought worthy of the highest praise?" Isocrates answers the question by citing bravery and military prowess.

Should he not clearly be loved by the gods and esteemed among men both for himself and for his good fortune? So then, perhaps it is better to give an overall account of your many virtues later, but I will try to present truthfully the praise I have for each of these qualities. [10] I will start by praising first that quality which is recognized at the outset by all who see you, your beauty, and in particular your complexion, thanks to which your limbs and whole body stand out. In considering what suitable image I can use for comparison, I cannot see one, and so it occurs to me to entreat those who read this speech to look at and examine you, so that I might be forgiven for saying that I have nothing to compare. [11] To what could you compare something mortal that creates an immortal desire in those who see it, the sight of which never satisfies, which is remembered when it is gone, and which in human form has a nature worthy of the gods, a flower in its loveliness, and without any hint of shame? Moreover, not even those criticisms that were leveled against many others who shared in beauty before now can be brought against your beauty. [12] For either through laziness they have ruined the overall allure of their person or some misfortune has affected their natural attractions as well. We would not find your beauty affected by any of these flaws, for whichever of the gods looked out for your person [12] at that time guarded so keenly against all such defects that you would merit no criticism, and in most respects your appearance would be most attractive. [13] Also, since the face is a person's most striking physical feature, and in the face the eyes [are most striking], even more in these did the divinity show the kind disposition he had to you. For not only did he give you excellent vision, but, since the virtue of some men cannot even be discerned from their feats, he made clear the most honorable qualities of your character through the evidence of your looks, making you seem gentle and kind to those who see you, noble and dignified to those who talk to you, and brave and prudent to all. [14] And a special cause for wonder is that although other men are assumed to be mean because of their gentleness, and arrogant because of their dignity, and seem overbearing because of their courage, and inane because of their silence, as far as you are concerned Fortune [13]

---

[12] The gods take care to promote Evagoras' ambitions in the same way in Isoc. 9.25.

[13] On Fortune, see *Letter* 1.13 and *Letter* 4.3.

has taken those qualities that oppose each other and has set them all in the necessary concord, as if answering a prayer or wanting to make an example for others but not, as is usual, creating an ordinary mortal.

[**15**] Therefore, if it were possible to describe your beauty in words, or if this were your only worthy feature, we would not need to mention your other qualities, but as it is, I am afraid that the listeners would be worn out from hearing the rest of these, and we would drag out our description in vain. [**16**] For how could someone exaggerate your beauty in a speech, when not even works of art executed by the skill of the best artists can exceed it?[14] Not that that is a surprise, for works of art have a static appearance, so that it is unclear how they would appear if they were alive, but the character of your mind elevates the extreme beauty of your body in everything you do. Therefore, I have praised your beauty only to this extent, and I have omitted many other qualities.

[**17**] As for your good conduct, I can make the highest compliment: that at your young age people easily incur criticism, but you have succeeded in being praised. For not only have you not made any mistakes but also you have chosen to live more sensibly than people of your age. And the way you interact with other men is the greatest proof of this; for although you encounter men who have all manner of characters and who all, moreover, try to coax you into a close friendship, you have managed such people so well that all have been pleased to be your friend. [**18**] This is a sign of those who choose to live honorably and humanely. And yet before now some people have been esteemed who have advised that the company of casual acquaintances should be avoided, or who have been persuaded by these men. For they claim that either one must be gracious to those who are immoral and so be slandered by many, or if they guard against such criticism, they must incur the dislike of those acquaintances themselves. [**19**] Although others think it is an impossible thing to please men who are different in many ways, I think that you must be praised even more so because you are so superior to them that you have prevailed over all the difficult and bad-tempered people, not granting others any reason to

---

[14] It was common to compare the beauty of the body with that of a statue (cf. Isoc. 9.73), an analogy made by Plato (*Phaedrus* 275d).

suspect you had improper relations with any, and overcoming their displeasure by the easy disposition of your ways.

[20] And so with your lovers, if one must also talk about these, you seem to me to consort with them so finely and modestly that although most people cannot act with restraint towards the one they have chosen, you are able to please everyone greatly. This is a clear sign of your virtue. For not one of your lovers does not receive from you what is just and right, and not one has any expectation of getting what causes shame, such is the extent of your modesty towards those who desire the best things, and such is the discouragement it provides to those who want to throw off all restraint. [21] Furthermore, most men when they are young preserve a reputation for modesty by their silence, but you so outdo them by your nature that you create no less of a reputation about yourself by what you say and do with your friends than by all the rest of your qualities, such is your power of persuasion and grace whether you are serious or are joking. For you are naïve but avoid mistakes, and clever but not malevolent, and generous but independent. In a nutshell, you are what a son of Virtue fathered by Eros would be.[15]

[22] And so to courage—for it is not right to leave this out. It is not that your character does not have the potential for great enhancement, or that the future will not yield more examples for those who want to praise you in speeches, but praise is most fitting for your youthful age, in which others only hope to do no wrong. But someone might describe your courage in many other areas, but especially your athletic training, for which there are also many witnesses. [23] Perhaps it is necessary to say first that you have done well to choose this kind of contest. For to decide correctly what one should do when one is a young man is a sign of a good mind and sound thinking, and on both accounts it would be wrong not to praise your choice.

Therefore, you are aware that slaves and foreigners share in the other competitions,[16] but only citizens have the right to take part in the

---

[15] Eros, god of sexual love, was the companion of Aphrodite, goddess of sexual love.

[16] Only freeborn Greeks could take part in the Olympic Games. The same was true for games held locally, but perhaps this rule was not as rigorously enforced, especially by the fourth century. The reference here is probably to the use of slave jockeys and charioteers in the equestrian events: see Golden 1998, p. 3.

dismounting contest,[17] and the best make it their goal, so you devoted yourself to this contest. [24] And yet judging that those who train for foot races acquire nothing towards their courage or spirit, and that those who train to box and such things corrupt their body and mind, you selected the noblest and grandest of competitions, the one that is especially appropriate for your nature, is most similar to warfare in its habitual use of arms and arduous effort in running, and in the magnificence and grandeur of its equipment resembles the power of the gods.[18] [25] In addition r ɔ hese, it presents a pleasurable spectacle, is composed of the most varied aspects, and is considered worthy of the greatest prizes. For in addition to those that are awarded, the training and practice for this event will seem no small prize even for those who aspire to virtue only in moderation.[19] Someone might make

---

[17] Harpocration, s.v. *apobates* (dismounting competition) says that this game took place in only Attica and Boeotia, but the competition is found at the Amphiaraia games in Oropus (*IG* vii 417, line 66, though this is later). The *apobates* was unique among the chariot races, for competitors, who were clad in armor, seem to have dismounted from their chariots during the race, and run alongside their team of horses before jumping back onto their chariots (*contra* Dionysius Halicarnassus 7.73.3, who says that they raced the length of the stadium on foot, but this seems unlikely): see Crowther 1991; cf. Clavaud in the Budé Text, pp. 135–137, and Golden 1998, p. 3. See also 25 and 28 with notes.

The speaker goes on to stress how superior physically and morally this competition was over other sports, such as running and boxing (24–25), as well as how thrilling such a spectacular sport must have been (28). There is a vivid description of Orestes' chariot race in Sophocles, *Electra* 680–763, and cf. Nestor's advice on charioteering at Homer, *Iliad* 23.310–350. On chariot racing, see Harris 1972, pp. 151–183.

[18] The gods habitually used chariots, and some such as Poseidon and Ares always had their own chariots.

[19] Crowther 1991, p. 175 n. 8, notes that in the classical period the prize was unknown but that at the later festivals the winner received one of the smallest monetary prizes offered. He also says that there is no reference to the event or its prize in *IG* ii² 2311, which lists competitions and prizes. However, that inscription is so fragmented that there may well have been a citation of the *apobates* that has been lost. If the prize was a material one, such as money or an amphora, it may well have been small, and the actual honor of winning was the "real" prize. On the other hand, the passage may even indicate that there was no actual prize but only

the poetry of Homer the best evidence for this, for he presents the Greeks and the barbarians making war against one another with this equipment.[20] And it is still the custom today to use it in the contests in the greatest cities of Greece, not the humblest.[21]

[26] So noble and so esteemed by all mankind is your choice. And considering that it is no use to want to set the highest goals or to have a good body in all respects, unless the soul has been prepared with ambition, you immediately showed industriousness in gymnastic training, nor did you fail in real contests but demonstrated the complete excellence of your nature and the courage of your soul in the games. [27] I am reluctant to begin speaking about this, for I might not do justice in this speech to what happened at that time. Nevertheless, I will not leave it out. For it is shameful not to want to report on what thrills us as spectators.

If I were to recount all your contests, perhaps I would make this account unacceptably long. But by relating one example in which you excelled, I will achieve the same effect but will be seen as making a more moderate use of my audience's patience. [28] When the teams had set off, and some had overtaken you and others were being reined in, you overcame both groups, in a manner appropriate to each case, and seized victory, taking that crown in such a way that although the victory was spectacular it seemed more wonderful and surprising that you survived. For when the chariot of your opponents was coming close to you,[22] and everyone thought the power of their horses

---

recognition of the winner's virtue, which transcended all material gains. Thus, according to the speaker, the people at the time realized how valuable the training for the event was and how high the quality of those who competed in it. (I thank Professor Golden for his email comments on this note.)

[20] Homeric heroes used chariots to convey them to battles, then dismounted to fight the enemy on foot while the drivers kept the chariot at a safe but close distance (e.g., Homer, *Iliad* 3.29, 6.103, 12.81, 13.385, 16.712–867).

[21] A reference to Athens and to Thebes. Alexander the Great razed Thebes to the ground in 335: see the Introduction. This reference dates the work before then.

[22] As Crowther 1991, p. 175, notes, the phrase "chariot of the opponents" suggests that there was more than one person in the chariot, the dismounter and a driver, who presumably steered the chariot as in Homeric times (see above). The speaker, however, refers to Epicrates as being solely responsible for dismounting

was beyond restraint, you saw that some of the other drivers were overreacting although there was no real danger, but you did not panic or act the coward, but by your courage you regained control of the momentum of your team, and by your speed overtook even those opponents who were enjoying better luck. [**29**] Moreover, you radically changed men's thinking, for although it is often said that in equestrian contests the finest sight is a crash, and they seem to speak the truth in this, in your case on the contrary all the spectators were afraid that you might have such a misfortune.[23] Your character led them to feel goodwill and to desire your success.

[**30**] Quite rightly, too. For it is an honor to become renowned for some one quality but much better to combine all those qualities of which any sensible man would be proud. This will be clear from the following. For we will find that the gods loved Aeacus and Rhadamanthys[24] because of their wisdom, Heracles,[25] Castor, and Pollux[26] because of their courage, and Ganymede, Adonis,[27] and others such as them because of their beauty. Consequently, I am not astonished at those who desire to be your friend, but rather at those who do not. For when some were considered worthy of associating with the gods

---

and driving the chariot, and so either this is poetic license or the driver was called upon only when the dismounter was out of the chariot. If the latter, then the dismounter would have concentrated only on running and getting back into the chariot. Another alternative (suggested by the anonymous referee of this volume) is that the phrase could be plural because charioteer and owner of the chariot were often different people, both thought of as opponents.

[23] Cf. the spectators' reaction to the tragic accident of Orestes at Sophocles, *Electra* 680–763.

[24] Aeacus was the father of Peleus and grandfather of Achilles. Rhadamanthys and his brother Minos were judges in the Underworld and were often cited together for their justice; e.g., by Plato, *Apology* 41a and *Gorgias* 524a–e; cf. Isoc. 9.14–15 (Aeacus).

[25] Heracles, son of Zeus and Alcmena, was famous for his twelve labors, on completion of which he became a god; see too *Funeral Oration* 8 and 31 with nn.

[26] Castor and Pollux (the Greek name is Polydeuces), the "Dioscuri," were twin sons of Zeus and Leda.

[27] Ganymede was so beautiful that Zeus carried him up to Olympus and he became the cupbearer of the gods. Adonis was loved by Aphrodite, and on his death (perhaps in a boar hunt) he was deified.

because they had one or another of the qualities I just mentioned, surely any human being would wish to become the friend of the possessor of all these qualities. [31] Therefore, when you so eclipse your peers in virtue, it is right that your father and mother and your other relatives are envied, and even more so those whom you, who are thought worthy of such great blessings, have chosen from all the rest to be friends. The former are associated with you by fortune but the latter are brought together with you by their own good and noble qualities. [32] I do not know whether I should call them lovers or only persons who think rightly. For it seems to me that even from the beginning, Fortune despised the ignoble and wanted to arouse the minds of good men and made your nature beautiful, not so that you would be deceived into hedonistic practices but so you would enjoy the benefits of virtue.

[33] I have still much to relate about you, but I think I will abandon my praise here, for I fear that my description of you will exceed the limits of human nature. For words, it seems, have much less power than sight, so that while no one would think to distrust what can be seen, people think that praise is untrue even when it fails to match the reality. [34] Therefore, I will stop speaking about this, and will try to advise you how you might make your life even more honored. I would like you to pay attention to what I am about to say and not treat it as unimportant; and do not think that I am addressing these words to you not for your own sake but because I wish to show my rhetorical skill. I do not want you to stray from the truth and choose random advice instead of the best, thereby doing yourself an injustice. [35] For we do not criticize those who have an undistinguished and lowly nature, even when they do something wrong, but those like you who have gained renown earn disgrace even by failing to do something honorable. And again, those who falsely interpret speeches about other matters make a poor judgment in one case only, but those who reject or despise advice for their general conduct have reminders of their own stupidity for all their life.

[36] You must not let any of this happen but consider what has the greatest influence in human affairs, what success would bring the greatest benefit, and what failure would do the most damage throughout life. For it is clear that we must pay the greatest attention to what has the most influence in tipping our lives one way or the other. [37] Accordingly, we will find that the mind controls all aspects of

human beings, and that philosophy alone has the power to educate and train it properly. So that is what I think you must study, and not hesitate or flee from the hard work it involves. Understand that through idleness and laziness even simple goals are difficult to achieve, but through endurance and industry nothing good is unattainable. [38] The most foolish thing of all is to be ambitious and to endure many adversities for the sake of wealth and strength and such things, which are all ephemeral and usually are slaves to the mind, rather than seeking ways to improve your mind, which controls everything else, and remains with those who have it to the end and sets the course for one's entire life. [39] And yet while it is a fine thing to be admired for great deeds that result from Fortune, it is far more honorable to take part in highly regarded matters thanks to one's own diligence. Even ignoble men have sometimes happened to share in the former, but no one can share in the latter except those who are exceptionally virtuous.

[40] Now, as far as philosophy goes, I think that there will be a more fitting opportunity for me in the future to review each point in detail, but nothing stops me speaking briefly about it now. First, you must understand this one point clearly, that all education comes from knowledge and practice, and philosophy more than any other, for the wiser its teachers are, the more finely does it combine them. [41] So since the mind manages speaking and deliberating, and philosophy gives us skill in each of these areas,[28] why would we not want to pursue this study, which will give us power in both? For it is probable that our life will make the greatest progress only when we set our sights on the most important goals and can attain those that are teachable by art, and the remainder by practice and habit. [42] For surely we cannot say that it is not by gaining knowledge that we surpass each other in understanding; in general, every nature grows better from receiving the right education, and most especially those that from the start were blessed with more natural talents than the others, for the former can only make themselves better but the latter can become superior to all others.

---

[28] Cf. Isoc. 15.266: "I do not, however, think it proper to apply the term 'philosophy' to a training which is no help to us in the present either in our speech or in our actions."

DEMOSTHENES.

DEMOSTHENES, SPEECHES 60 AND 61, PROLOGUES,
LETTERS; TRANS. BY IAN WORTHINGTON.
                Paper   142 P.

AUSTIN: UNIVERSITY OF TEXAS PRESS, 2006
SER: ORATORY OF CLASSICAL GREECE; V. 10.

NEW TRANSLATION OF WORKS OF ATTIC ORATOR AND
STATESMAN WITH INTRO. AND NOTES.
LCCN 2006-11488

ISBN 0292713320   LIB PO#

                                  PA3951

LIST	19.95
DISC	5.0%
NET	18.95

    9473 BATES COLLEGE   1090-08
DATE 1/31/07 NEH

YBP - CONTOOCOOK, N.H. 03229

SUBJ: DEMOSTHENES--TRANSLATIONS INTO ENGLISH.

CLASS PA3951   DEWEY# 885.01   LEVEL ADV-AC

[43] Understand that experience gained from practice is perilous and has no value for the rest of one's life, but education based on philosophy is the right blend for all these occasions. To be sure, some men before now through their training have been admired because of the good fortune attendant on their actions, but it is fitting that you should treat these people with disdain and look to improving yourself. For you must not act impulsively in the most important matters, but only out of knowledge, and when a situation arises, you must not need to practice but must know how best to enter the fray.

[44] Consider that all philosophy confers great benefits on those who practice it, and most especially the knowledge of practical matters and political discourses. It is disgraceful to be ignorant of geometry and other such disciplines, but to become a top contender is well below your worth; in philosophy, however, you should strive to excel, but to be completely ignorant would be laughable. [45] There are many ways in which you might know this, and especially from examining those men who became renowned before your time. You will hear how Pericles,[29] who was considered to eclipse all men of his time in wisdom, studied with Anaxagoras of Clazomenae,[30] and as his pupil acquired this power. And you will find that Alcibiades,[31] whose nature was far worse than his virtue, elected to live his life arrogantly, subserviently, and excessively, but through his association with Socrates he made much of his life right and hid the remainder by the greatness of his other deeds. [46] But if we should not waste time talking about those in the past when we can use more recent examples, then you will find that Timotheus[32] was

---

[29] On Pericles, the great fifth-century Athenian general and statesman, see Kagan 1991.

[30] An important presocratic philosopher, the first from overseas to live in Athens. He was later indicted by Pericles' enemies and fled to Lampsacus. The relationship between Pericles and Anaxagoras is also noted by Isoc. 15.235; Plato, *Phaedrus* 270a; Plut., *Pericles* 4.6.

[31] On Alcibiades, a brilliant but controversial fifth-century general, see Andoc. 4 and Lys. 14 (translated in this series); see further Bloedow 1973 and Kagan 1981.

[32] Timotheus was an outstanding Athenian general of the 370s and 360s. In 356 he was one of the commanders in the Social War (see *Prologue* 2.3). His alleged bungling led to his trial, and he was fined the huge amount of one hundred talents, which forced him to flee to Chalcis, where he died two or three years

considered worthy of the greatest repute and highest honors not because of what he did as a young man but for his accomplishments after studying with Isocrates. And Archytas of Tarentum,[33] who as ruler of that city administered affairs so well and philanthropically that his record spread to all and sundry, was at first despised and only gained great distinction after his association with Plato. [47] And none of these things came about without reason,[34] for it would be much stranger if we had to realize small goals through learning and practice but could achieve the greatest without this trouble.

I do not know what more I should say about these things, for I did not introduce them at the start because I considered you completely ignorant about them, but I thought that exhortations like these encourage the ignorant and inspire those who know. [48] And do not suppose that in saying this I am offering to teach you any of it myself, for I am not ashamed to say that I still need to learn much, and I have chosen to compete in the political arena rather than teach others. By making this clarification, I am not demeaning the reputation of those who choose to teach wisdom, but the truth of the matter is as follows: [49] I know well that many men from ignoble and low backgrounds have become illustrious through this discipline and that Solon[35] earned the highest reputation both in his lifetime and after he died. He was not excluded from other honors, but left a testimonial to his courage in

---

later. He was one of Isocrates' more celebrated students; cf. Isoc. 15.101–140, from which passage, as Clavaud suggests in the Budé text, the author of the essay has extracted his reference to Timotheus.

[33] According to Diogenes Laertius (8.79–83), Archytas was a Pythagorean, whose virtue (*aretē*) and military excellence led to his election as a general seven times when the local law forbade reelection. He was apparently in control of Tarentum when Plato went to Sicily in 338 (Plato, *Letter* 7.326b), although it is unknown if he was one of his pupils.

[34] Cf. Isoc. 4.150, where the Greek is almost identical.

[35] There is similar praise of Solon in Isoc. 15.231–232 and 235, on which the author may be drawing. He is often called "the father of democracy" because his political legislation in 594/3 was to end the monopoly of power exercised by influential nobles and eventually allowed Athens to become a democracy. See further Forrest 1966, pp. 143–174; Andrewes 1974, pp. 78–91.

the trophy of victory over the Megarians,[36] [50] to his statesmanship in the recovery of Salamis, and to his wisdom in his laws, which even today most Greeks continue to uphold.[37] Nevertheless, with all these grand accomplishments, nothing did he work harder to achieve than becoming one of the Seven Sages;[38] for he realized that philosophy brought honor not infamy to those who practiced it, and his judgment in this matter was no less sound than in other matters in which he was preeminent.

[51] My judgment is no different, and I advise you to study philosophy, bearing in mind the advantages you begin with. I myself discussed them at the start of my essay,[39] not because I expected to win you over by my praise of your nature but in order that I might exhort you more to philosophy, provided you do not disparage it, and give less thought to future advantages through pride in those which you already possess. [52] Even if you are superior to ordinary men, do not stop trying to outdo the others, but make it your highest goal to be first among all,[40] for you will gain more from being seen to be striving for this goal than from being preeminent among ordinary men. And do not debase your character, do not cheat of their hopes those who think highly of you, but try by your own strength to exceed the wishes of those who think the most of you. [53] Consider further that other speeches that are just bring credit to the writers, but wise advice confers benefits and honor on those who are persuaded by it; and decisions about other matters make clear the understanding that we have, but choosing a career tests our whole character. So, when you decide

---

[36] Megara's seizure of Nisaea (which became its port) and Salamis from the Athenians led to Athens waging a successful war for their recovery, perhaps at the end of the seventh century. Solon's role in this war cannot be gauged with certainty.

[37] There is rhetorical exaggeration here as Greeks outside Athens had their own laws. Solon's laws were inscribed on wooden beams (*axones*) set up in the Agora, and later they were reinscribed onto bronze or stone blocks (*kyrbeis*); see further Rhodes 1981, pp. 131–135.

[38] Literally "the Seven Sophists," which is an unusual expression and most likely taken from Isoc. 15.235. The legend of the Seven Sages arose only in the fourth century: see Plato, *Protagoras* 343a.

[39] See 10–32.

[40] For similar advice, cf. Isoc. 9.81.

about this, expect at the same time to be judged by all men.[41] And I, who have so willingly praised you, will also have a stake in your test. [54] The same things that make you seem worthy of my praises must excuse me for my friendship with you.

I should not so earnestly call you to philosophy[42] if I did not think that this was the best illustration I could make to show my goodwill for you, and if I had not observed that because of the dearth of good and noble men,[43] the city often relies on ordinary men, and because of their errors falls into the direst misfortunes. [55] Therefore, I have more strenuously exhorted you so that the city may enjoy your virtue and you enjoy the honors it bestows. In fact, I do not think that you will be allowed to live at fortune's whim, but that the city will call upon you to administer some of its affairs, and the more illustrious your nature, the more it will consider you worthy of accomplishing, and the sooner it will want to put you to the test. Thus, it is good to train your mind so that you will not be found wanting when the time comes.

[56] It has been my task to tell you what I think it would be best for you to do; your task is to decide about it. And others also who seek to be your friend should not be content with superficial gratifications and pastimes, or to exhort you to enjoy these, but should work hard and consider how they might make your life as illustrious as possible. In that way, they would earn the greatest praise for themselves and would be responsible for the greatest benefits for you. [57] Not that I find any fault now with those who associate with you, for this seems to me to be one factor in your general good fortune, that you have had no disreputable lover but pick friends from among your group that anyone would gladly choose. I advise you, however, while remaining friendly and agreeable to all of these, to be influenced by those who have the most sense, in order that you may seem even better to these men and to the rest of the citizens. Good luck.

---

[41] This is a common appeal in forensic oratory. Din. 1.3, e.g., also warns the jury that it will be judged by its verdict: "You should consider, Athenians, that just as this man Demosthenes is on trial before you, so are you before your peers."

[42] The same Greek expression occurs at Isoc. 6.87, except that "philosophy" is replaced by "war."

[43] *Kalos kagathos:* see 1n10.

PROLOGUES

〜〜〜〜〜〜〜〜〜〜〜〜〜〜〜〜〜〜〜〜〜〜〜〜〜〜〜〜〜〜〜〜〜〜〜〜〜〜〜

INTRODUCTION

The following are prologues to political speeches delivered in the Assembly.[1] Here, citizens over the age of 18 debated and voted on all matters of domestic and foreign policy. An Assembly meeting started at about dawn and lasted until the mid-afternoon. An agenda was carefully worked through, proposals were put to the people and speeches made for and against them (in theory, anyone had the right to speak); they were discussed and voted on by a show of hands.[2] A majority vote carried the proposal.

Classical rhetorical theory divided a speech into four sections: prologue (*prooimion*), narration (*diēgēsis*), proof (*pistis*), and conclusion (*epilogos*). In this arrangement (*taxis*), each section had its own distinct role. Of the prologue, Aristotle tells us that it was like "the prologue in poetry and the prelude in flute-playing; for all these are beginnings, and as it were a paving the way for what follows" (*Rhetoric* 3.14.1). Hence, the prologue was more than a mere opening: it foreshadowed what was to come and had the important rhetorical function of gaining the goodwill of the audience (*captatio benevolentiae*) from the outset.[3]

---

[1] Only 55 of the 56 are actual prologues of speeches as Number 54 is an account of state sacrifices performed in honor of various gods in order to protect the city's safety. It was wrongly included in the collection of prologues.

[2] On the Assembly, see Hansen 1991.

[3] For lengthy discussions by the classical rhetoricians of the use of prologues in all types of speeches, see Arist., *Rhetoric* 3.14; Anaximenes, *Rhetorica ad Alexandrum* 29; and Quintilian 4.1; cf.Cicero, *de Oratore* 2.80. For some general remarks,

Moreover, often in no more than a dozen or two lines, multiple themes were lucidly outlined, and the audience was advised what to do. The prologue was also meant to balance the conclusion to a speech, which summarized the case and attempted to persuade the audience to be well disposed to the speaker (Arist., *Rhetoric* 3.19.1, Anaximenes, *Rhetorica ad Alexandrum* 36).

The prologue was meant to capture the goodwill of the audience. Hence, it is plausible to assume that the information contained in them is accurate, for speakers would not wish to incur their audience's enmity. Equally as important as the prologues' rhetorical value, then, is their historical value: they give us insights into the Athenians' attitude to their democracy as well as to the reactions and even expectations of the audience at an Assembly. The *Prologues* often criticize the speakers and the shortcomings of the people in the Athenian democracy. This, however, is in keeping with their theme that democracy is the best form of government. The criticisms are meant to stress the responsibilities of both sides.

We also have glimpses of the restlessness of the people and their penchant to heckle speakers who talked for too long (21.1, 36, 46), of their boredom from listening to speeches (29.3, 34.2), and of their quickness in forcing speakers not to go off at tangents (56). There was probably not a great deal of time to deal with all the business in hand, and we can expect a fair degree of impatience on the part of speakers anxious to speak and of listeners anxious to vote and leave. Some of the prologues indicate that hasty decisions were sometimes made because of the rushed order of business (18 and 21).

Of interest is the level of decorum expected in an Assembly. In a court of law, abuse of opponents was accepted, but this was frowned upon in the Assembly, even though the same people who sat as jurors attended the Assembly. Attitude was something that these *Prologues* clearly address. Not only should there be no personal abuse against other speakers in a speech (11, 20, 31, 52, 53.1–2), but also such practice is a disservice to the people and reflects badly against the speaker himself (6, 31, 53.1–2).

---

cf. Usher 1999, pp. 22–23, and see especially de Brauw 2006, and Yunis 1996, pp. 247–257.

While the prologues are mentioned incidentally in works dealing with Demosthenes and Greek oratory, they have never been the subject of a dedicated study in English and have been unjustly neglected.[4] The reader is directed to my article cited in note 4 for further information on them and the light they cast on the relationship between speaker and audience.

The authorship of the prologues is disputed. Callimachus, who collected them for the Library at Alexandria, believed that Demosthenes composed them, as did Pollux and Stobaeus. Modern scholars are divided but lean heavily toward authenticity;[5] for more discussion, see my article. There is a possibility that they were merely rhetorical exercises, but I do not agree. There is no question that Demosthenes had the rhetorical expertise to write them, and some of them are certainly similar in style to his deliberative speeches. Thus, Number 1 corresponds very closely to the opening of Dem. 4 (*Philippic* 1), Number 3 to Dem. 1 (*Olynthiac* 1), while Number 7 is almost exactly the opening of Dem. 14 (*On the Symmories*), Number 27 of Dem. 15 (*For the Liberty of the Rhodians*), and Number 8 of Dem. 16 (*For the People of Megalopolis*). We also have several prologues that correspond to only parts of Demosthenes' speeches (these are pointed out where they occur).

The majority of the prologues bear no relation to Demosthenes' other extant speeches. However, we have only seventeen public speeches by him (1–17), and there is no question that he delivered more in over thirty years of high-profile public life.[6] Moreover, it does not follow that because we have 55 prologues proper there must have been 55 actual speeches. It is possible that Demosthenes had several prologues on hand to meet a particular situation. He may have written out his

---

[4] Early specific studies are by Swoboda 1887 and Rupprecht 1927. Clavaud in the Budé Text has an excellent discussion, and see now Worthington 2004b.

[5] Swoboda (1887) rejected them, but those who believe they are Demosthenic include Blass 1898, pp. 281–287; Dobson 1919, p. 267; Rupprecht 1927, pp. 365–432; Goldstein 1968, pp. 13–24; and Clavaud in the Budé Text. Kennedy (1963, p. 53) is noncommittal, and the DeWitts in the Loeb edition have nothing to say on the matter.

[6] We have no speeches from when Alexander was king (336–323), but we know that Demosthenes spoke in the Assembly: see Worthington 2000.

speeches before an Assembly at which he knew he would speak on a specific matter (for example, resistance to Philip). However, there must have been times in a debate when he had to speak on an issue for which he was unprepared. Plutarch tells us that Demosthenes was not adept at extemporaneous speaking (*Demosthenes* 8.2, 10.1) and that the audience's noise made him anxious (*Demosthenes* 6.3, 8.7). Indeed, he had to develop his own manner of delivery and speaking in order to find favor in the Assembly.[7] Therefore, it would make sense for him to have several prologues to meet any occasion and to choose one to lead off a speech.

To note the many similarities in the language and contents of each prologue (for example, the plea that the people must listen in order to cast an informed vote, which is found in 3, 4, 5, and 47) would generate a vast number of cross-references and thus notes, and so I do not do this. Readers will be able to recognize similarities and "themes" easily enough.

PROLOGUES

I

[**1**] Gentlemen of Athens,[8] if the subject proposed for discussion had been some new matter, I would have waited until most of the usual speakers had declared their opinions,[9] and if anything they said pleased me, I would have kept quiet; otherwise, only then would I have tried to state my own opinion. But since you are now contemplating matters about which these men have spoken many times before, I believe that although I am rising first I might reasonably be seen as speaking after them. [**2**] If our affairs were prospering, it would not be necessary to deliberate, but since they are in a bad way, as all of you can see, on this basis I will attempt to advise you on what I

---

[7] See further Cooper 2004.

[8] Sections 1–2 correspond very closely to the first section of Dem. 4, *Philippic* 1, of 351.

[9] In an Assembly the herald asked if anyone over the age of fifty wished to speak first, and younger men would then follow them (cf. Aes. 1.23). This prologue seems to suggest that the speaker was a young man, hence he has to justify why he is speaking first; cf. Dem. 4.1, and note the far more critical *Prologue* 13.

consider the best course of action. First, then, you must understand that nothing you were doing during the war[10] must be done in the future, but rather the exact opposite. For if those policies have made you weak, opposite ones are likely to make things better. [3] Next, you must not think that the speaker who makes little or no demand on you is right, for you can see how such hopes and advice have caused our present total ruin, but rather it is the speaker who refuses to try to please you[11] and says what must be done and how we may end incurring such shameful losses. To speak truthfully: if a speaker wants to avoid causing you pain and passes over something in a speech that will also be passed over in the course of events, he should speak to please you, but if the allure of words is not fitting for the occasion and causes actual harm, then it is disgraceful to deceive yourselves, and to wait until absolutely compelled before doing what you should willingly have done long before.[12]

2

[1] I do not have the same thoughts, gentlemen of Athens, when I hear the name you give to our constitution and when I see the way that some of you treat those who speak on its behalf. You call our constitution a democracy, as you all know, but I see some listening favorably to those who oppose it.[13] [2] I wonder what their motive can be. Do you think they say this without recompense? The leaders of oligarchies, on

---

[10] Probably the war against Philip II of 357–346. A possible context for this prologue is the 344–342 period when the Peace of Philocrates of 346 was breaking down and Philip's activities, especially in the Chersonese, were a source of grave concern to the Athenians.

[11] Cf. Dem. 3.3, 4.38, and 9.63–64 on the orators who try only to please their audience.

[12] Clavaud in the Budé Text believes that the speaker refers to the requests for Athenian troops from Olynthus in 349/8 when Philip II invaded the Chalcidice. Demosthenes urged Athenian assistance in his three *Olynthiac* speeches. However, the similarity between this prologue and *Philippic* 1 of 351 suggests a date earlier than 348.

[13] That is, who advocate oligarchy. This criticism of those who oppose democracy is common in prologues; cf. the Introduction to *Prologues,* and also *Funeral Oration* 25.

whose behalf these men are speaking, may well give them more on the side.[14] Have you decided that what they say is better than the others? Then oligarchy looks better to you than democracy! Do you think the speakers are better men? Who could you reasonably consider honorable, when he speaks publicly against the established constitution? I conclude that you must be mistaken when you hold this opinion. Gentlemen of Athens, be on your guard lest you fall into the trap of ever giving an opportunity to those plotting against you, for you will only discover your mistake when it will not be of any use to you.[15] [3] Gentlemen of Athens, it is perhaps not surprising that everything is not going as we would wish, for either ourselves or our allies.[16] For the accident of Fortune (*tychē*) prevails over many things, and there are many reasons why everything does not work out according to expectation. We are only human. But for the people to share in nothing at all when their opponents have everything, gentlemen of Athens, that, in my view, is astonishing and frightening to sensible men. This is the starting point of my entire speech.

3

Gentlemen of Athens,[17] I believe that you would all give a great deal of money for advice that would be of benefit to you in the matters you are now discussing. That being the case, it is proper for you to listen willingly to those who want to advise you. For if someone comes here having worked out a beneficial plan, not only would you listen and

---

[14] It is possible that Demosthenes has in mind here his personal and political rival Aeschines, whom he often accused of being in the pay of Philip (see, e.g., 21.1n). See further on the two and their rivalries: Buckler 2000.

[15] The Oxford Classical Text of Rennie and the Budé Text print the following section (3) as a separate prologue, following the earlier edition of Blass (1893).

[16] The Athenians' allies are those in their Second Athenian Naval Confederacy, founded in 378 and disbanded by Philip after Chaeronea: see Cargill 1981. In 356 Chios, Byzantium, and Rhodes led a revolt that, despite Athenian military intervention (cf. *Letter* 3.31), was successful. When it ended in 355, many allies defected from the confederacy. Dem. 15.3 tells us that the Athenians were accused of plotting against these three states, which led to their defection.

[17] The opening of Dem. 1, *Olynthiac* 1, of 348 is very similar.

adopt it, but also I consider it your good fortune that some will propose many beneficial suggestions on the spur of the moment, so that your choice of what is expedient from all of them will be easier.

4

Gentlemen of Athens, since it is in your hands to choose whichever proposal you wish, it is right that you listen to all of them. For it often happens that the same man speaks incorrectly about one thing but not another; so that by shouting him down when you are annoyed with him you may lose many beneficial ideas, but by listening properly and quietly, you will adopt every good measure, and if you think someone is speaking stupidly you will ignore him. Now, I am not accustomed to making long speeches, and even if that had been my custom on a previous occasion, I would avoid it at this time, but I will tell you in as few words as I am able what I consider is in your best interest.

5

[1] I see, gentlemen of Athens, that it is entirely clear which speeches you listen to with pleasure and which you are not pleased to hear. Nevertheless, I consider that the mark of those who want to deceive you is to say what they think will please you, whereas I judge that the loyal and fair citizen is the one who will withstand your jeers and whatever else you wish to do and propose what he himself feels is in the best interests of the city. [2] I would like you to listen to the speeches of both sides if for no other reason than that if someone clearly proposes better advice than that which you are following, you may make use of it, but if he fails and is unable to get his message across, it will be clear that he suffered this failure through his own fault and not because you were unwilling to listen to him. Besides, it would not be so grievous if you listened at length to someone speaking nonsense as if you prevented from speaking someone who had something good to propose. [3] Thus, the start of judging any matter correctly is not to believe you know something before you learn, especially since you know that many men before now have changed their minds. Therefore, if you are now persuaded by this, I think that I myself may be judged to speak a few words reasonably in opposition and that my proposal may be seen to be the best.

6

Although many speeches have been delivered by all your advisers, gentlemen of Athens, I do not see that you are any closer now to discovering what must be done than before you came up to the Assembly.[18] I believe the reason for this is the same as for our general wretched plight: namely, that the speakers do not offer you advice about the present situation but accuse and ridicule each other, making you used to hearing, so I judge, without proper legal evaluation, all the crimes they commit in order that if they are brought to trial some day, you will think you are hearing nothing new but only what has many times made you angry, and will thus be more lenient jurors and judges of their actions.[19] Perhaps at this present time it is foolish to ask exactly why they do this, but because it is not in your best interests I condemn them for it. I will not accuse anyone today, nor will I make any claim that I cannot immediately demonstrate, nor will I do anything that these men generally do, but as quickly as I can, I will tell you what I think is the best policy for your circumstances and will benefit you who deliberate, and then I will step down.

7

[I] Gentlemen of Athens,[20] those who praise your ancestors seem to me to choose a flattering account, and yet they do not benefit those whom they praise.[21] For when taking it upon themselves to speak of deeds to which no man can do justice in a speech, they acquire the

---

[18] Literally "up" as the Assembly was held on top of a large rock, the Pnyx, close to the Acropolis. On the Assembly, see further Hansen 1991.

[19] The Athenians were quick to censure corruption on the part of their elected officials and advisers in the Assembly, and the death penalty could be inflicted on those found guilty of deception (Dem. 20.100, 135). See also *Prologues* 25.3, 29.3, 37.2, and note the harsh criticisms of generals at *Prologue* 40.

[20] This prologue is identical to the opening of Dem. 14, *On the Symmories,* of 354/3 (1–2).

[21] Praise of the Athenians' ancestors was a common *topos* in Greek oratory and of course fundamental to a funeral oration.

reputation of being powerful speakers themselves, but they make their audience think that the courage of those men is less than they supposed. I myself think that the greatest praise of those men is time: when a lengthy period has elapsed and no other men have been able to show greater deeds than those performed by those men. [**2**] I myself will try to tell you how I think you can best make preparations. It is like this: if all of us show ourselves to be skillful speakers, I know well that your affairs would be no better off; but if someone, whoever he is, comes forward and can instruct and persuade us about the preparations that will benefit the city, and their extent, and their sources of funding, then all our current fear is gone. I shall try to do this as far as I am able; but first let me briefly tell you my opinion about our relations with the King.[22]

8

[**1**] Both sides seem to me be in the wrong,[23] gentlemen of Athens, those who have spoken for the Arcadians and those for the Spartans.[24] For they are abusing and slandering one another just as if they came here from each of the two cities and were not part of you, whom both sides are petitioning. This was the task of the visiting envoys, but the duty of those who consider themselves worthy to advise here is to speak about matters impartially and to consider your own best interests without rivalry. [**2**] But as it is, if you take away the fact that they are

---

[22] This was the King of Persia. The context is perhaps the immediate aftermath of the Social War (see *Prologue* 2.3), when the Athenians were contemplating making war on Persia. Demosthenes, in his first public appearance in the Assembly, successfully argued against the war in *On the Symmories* (14): its opening is identical to this prologue. See further Badian 2000, pp. 28–30.

[23] This prologue is identical to the opening of Dem. 16, *For the People of Megalopolis*, of 353 (1–3).

[24] The probable context is the appeal from the Arcadians for Athenian help against the Spartans, who were intent on increasing their power. Both the Arcadians and Spartans sent embassies to Athens, and Demosthenes unsuccessfully spoke in favor of the Arcadians (16, *For the People of Megalopolis*). The opening is identical to this prologue. On the speech and context, see Badian 2000, pp. 30–31; Usher 1999, pp. 211–213.

known and speak the Attic dialect, I believe that many would think they were Arcadians or Spartans!

I myself know how hard it is to propose the best policy, for when you are deceived and some want this and others that, if someone attempts to propose a middle course and you do not wait to learn what he says, he will please neither side and will be criticized by both. [3] Nevertheless, I myself will prefer to be seen as talking nonsense, if that is my fate, than abandon you to the deception of others against what I consider are your best interests. Therefore, with your permission, I will speak about other points later and will begin my advice on what I consider is the best policy with what has been agreed to by both sides.

9

[1] I have stood up because I do not agree with the opinions of some of those who have spoken, gentlemen of Athens. However, I will not accuse these men of speaking against your best interests from malice. It is rather that many people neglect to judge things, but are accustomed to looking only at the words they will utter, and if they come up with plenty of these, they are ready to address the people. They are wrong to think this, and do not reflect that many deeds are performed by everyone over a long period of time, but because of circumstances some have not worked out, and if a speaker speaks of one type and ignores the other, he will without realizing it be falling into the easiest of traps, deceiving himself. [2] Therefore, those who engage in advising the people seem to me to consider that the reputation for speaking well which they get from their speeches is sufficient ambition. However, I think that the man who undertakes to advise the city on policy should rather consider how his proposals will be beneficial than how his present words will curry favor. For men who gain distinction by their speeches should add the execution of some beneficial deed in order that what they say will have worth not only now but always.

10

[1] Gentlemen of Athens, if you have decided what is the best course to pursue concerning the present situation, then it is wrong to propose the matter for debate. For why should you be bothered to

listen in vain to what you yourselves have considered is beneficial before hearing debate? But if you are considering and deliberating because you must decide on the basis of speeches, it is not right to prevent those wanting to speak, for in doing this you deprive yourselves wholly of the voices of some and of anything useful they have devised, and you make the others put aside their judgment and propose only what they think you desire to hear. [2] It is those who wish to do wrong who force the speaker to say what you desire, but those who deliberate will hear what he has in mind, consider it, and if it has value, adopt it. I say this not as someone about to offer a proposal in opposition to those that please you, but because I know that, if you do not want to listen to the opposition, they will say that you have been deceived, but if you listen and are not persuaded, they will have been proved then and there to be giving the worse advice.

II

I think all of you know, gentlemen of Athens, that you have come here today not to judge any criminals but to deliberate about the present situation. So then, we must put off all the accusations, and when we put someone on trial let each man then speak before you against whomever he is convinced is guilty.[25] But if someone has something useful or beneficial to say, speak it now. For accusation is for those who find a failing with the past, but deliberation is concerned with the present and future.[26] Therefore, the present time is not for ridicule or blame, but for advice, it seems to me. To this end, I will try to guard against falling into the trap for which I condemn others, and to advise what I consider the best policy for the present situation.

---

[25] The Assembly also had judicial functions in that it could judge certain major crimes, such as treason.

[26] As Aristotle tells us in the *Rhetoric* (1.3.4), forensic speeches were concerned with the past and with justice as opposed to deliberative speeches that, by their nature, addressed what needed to be done for the future (cf. Dem. 18.192: "No one proposes deliberation about the past: it is the present and the future that call the statesman to his post").

12

[**1**] Gentlemen of Athens, I believe that no one will dispute that it is the mark of an evil and malevolent man to hate or love those who enter pubic life so strongly that he thinks nothing of the best interests of the city, but gives his public speeches out of spite or friendship, as some of the speakers here are doing. To these men I would say only that I think that if they have done something along these lines, this is not their greatest crime, but that they show they are prepared never to stop doing it. [**2**] I advise you not to betray your interests and consider it sufficient to punish them when it seems right to you. Instead, to the best of your ability prevent them from doing it, and, as befits those deliberating on behalf of the city, do away with your private rivalries and decide on the best path for the common good. Understand that no one, not even all the politicians together, can be adequately punished once the laws on which you depend are destroyed.[27]

13

It may perhaps be invidious to some people, gentlemen of Athens, if a private citizen and one of the masses like you should come forward after others who stand out for their long political experience and high reputation among you, and should say that he thinks they speak not only incorrectly but also are not even close to knowing what must be done.[28] Nevertheless, I so firmly think that I will state a more beneficial policy than they that I do not hesitate to say their advice is of no value. I believe you would do well to consider not the speaker but his advice. For, gentlemen of Athens, you must show goodwill not just to a few because of their birth,[29] but to those who always speak the best advice.

---

[27] On Athens as a society subject to the rule of law, see Aes. 3.196–200. The rule of law is often praised in forensic oratory, where the jurors are constantly urged to remain true to their dicastic oath (which they swore annually), and vote in a fair and just way and so uphold the laws. For the oath, see Dem. 24.149–151.

[28] The object of the scorn here could be Aeschines.

[29] For a similar complaint, cf. *Prologue* 55.2.

14

[1] I would like you to listen attentively, gentlemen of Athens, to what I have to say, for this is no trifling matter. I am amazed at why it is that before we come up to the Assembly any one you might meet can easily say how the present circumstances can be improved, and then again as soon as you leave it is the same: each man will say what must be done. However, when we are gathered together here and are considering these matters, you hear everything but this from certain speakers. [2] Gentlemen of Athens, is it that each of you knows what must be done and can state the duties of others, but no one likes to contribute himself? Or again, does each of you in private criticize others and show himself ready to do what is best, but in public you refuse to vote in measures through which you will all do some public service[30] for the city? [3] Well then, if you think that no crisis will ever come to expose this hypocrisy, it would be fine to continue in this manner. However, if you see trouble approaching, you must see how you can avoid fighting close by against what you could guard against from a distance, and not let those whom you now ignore later revel over what you might suffer.

15

[1] Gentlemen of Athens, although the city's present affairs are not as they should be, it does not seem to me too hard to discover what action would make them better. However, I think it is troubling to know the way in which I must speak about them to you. It is not that you will not comprehend what someone might say, but you seem to me to have got so used to hearing numerous lies and everything but the best policies for your affairs that I am afraid lest the person who now speaks what is best will incur the enmity that you ought to feel for those who deceived you. [2] For I see that you often hate not those responsible for your troubles but those who spoke to you last about them.[31] Nevertheless, despite a careful reckoning up of these dangers,

---

[30] The Greek verb is *leitourgein,* "to perform a liturgy"; cf. *Prologue* 48.3. On liturgies, see *Letter* 2.12n27.

[31] Cf. Dem. 1.16 on the perils of speaking last in a debate.

I think I should omit everything else and say only what I consider the best course of action for our present troubles.

16

I should have wished that you, gentlemen of Athens, would treat yourselves with that same generosity which you usually show all others, but right now you are better at righting the troubles of others than in giving thought to the problems that afflict you. Perhaps someone might say that this in itself brings the greatest glory to a city: to choose to face many dangers for the sake of justice alone, not for any private gain. I myself consider this reputation about the city to be true and want it so, but I also take it for granted that the job of wise men is to have as much foresight about their own affairs as about those of others, in order that you will demonstrate not only manifest generosity but also that you are sensible.

17

Perhaps, gentlemen of Athens, it is right for someone who wants to give you advice to try to speak in such a way that you can agree with him, but if not, to disregard all the other topics and advise only on the situation at hand, and this in the fewest words possible. For it seems to me that it is not from any dearth of speeches that you now see all your affairs in ruin, but because some are speaking and acting publicly for their own gain, and others who have not yet shown evidence of this prefer to be considered clever speakers rather than to bring about some beneficial act by what they say. And in order that I do not contradict my own advice, and say more about other matters than those I stood up to discuss, I will ignore all other topics and will attempt to tell you what I advise.

18

It seems to me that you would rightly pay attention, gentlemen of Athens, if someone undertakes to show you that in the matter you are considering the same course is just and expedient. I myself think that I will do this without difficulty, if you will grant me a very small request.

Let no one of you who has an opinion about the present situation think that he is right in all respects, but if something happens to be said against him, let him consider it, listening patiently to everything. Then if it appears that something right has been said, adopt it. For the proposal that succeeds will belong to you who adopt it as much as to the speaker who proposed it.[32] Therefore, the correct way to begin considering matters is to decide before hearing the considerations on which you must base your decision. For the opportunity and the manner of confirming a decision are not the same as the first examination of what seems beneficial.

19

I have come forward to ask your advice, gentlemen of Athens, about whether I should speak or not. I will tell you why I am at a loss to decide this myself. It seems to me that the man who does not want to please himself or a few people but wishes to say on your behalf what he is sure is most beneficial, should out of necessity support what both sides say well and should oppose what he thinks they say unjustly. Therefore, if you should submit to listen to both sorts of arguments briefly, you would deliberate far better about the remaining issues, but if you ignore me before learning what I say, it will be my luck to be criticized by both sides without wronging either. It is not right that I should suffer in this way. Therefore, if you tell me to, I am willing to speak; otherwise it is better for me to be quiet.

20

[1] I believe it is both right and expedient for you, gentlemen of Athens, to set aside charges and recriminations when we are to deliberate, and for each man to say what he thinks is best in the present situation. For we all know that the actions of certain men are responsible for the sorry state of our affairs and the job of an adviser is to show you how they can be made better. [2] Moreover, I think that the severest accusers of those who do wrong are not those who inquire into past actions at

---

[32] For a similar view, see Thuc. 3.43.4–5.

times like these, when they will not pay any penalty, but those who can give the sort of advice that may improve the situation. Thanks to them, when you are at peace you may also be able to punish them. [3] Therefore, I think that all other arguments are superfluous, and I will try to say what I think is the expedient course in the matter under consideration. I ask only this: if I should mention some past act, do not consider that I do so in order to accuse anyone, but to show you your past mistakes in order to prevent you suffering the same fate again.

21

[1] If in the past, gentlemen of Athens, we had kept as quiet as now and had not followed any politician, I believe that recent events would not have arisen, and I think that you would be much better off in many respects. But through the rash actions of some men, it is not possible to come forward or speak or in general to utter a word.[33] [2] The consequences are many and perhaps unpleasant. If therefore you want things to remain always the same as now, listening to speakers, considering what to do, and suffering like then, vote as you did in the past, launch triremes, embark, pay a tax, all those sorts of things.[34] Then after three or five days, if reports of our enemies cease and they remain peaceful, you will again suppose that there is no longer a need to do anything.[35] This happened when we heard that

---

[33] The context is perhaps the Fourth Sacred War of 340–339 and its aftermath, in which case the "rash" action would be that of Aeschines. In 340 the Locrians of Amphissa attacked Athens in a meeting of the Amphictyonic Council (a council of Greek states that administered the oracle of Apollo at Delphi), but Aeschines was able to turn the tables on them for allegedly cultivating sacred land (Aes. 3.107–131; Dem. 18.150). A sacred war was declared on them, with Philip II in command of the Amphictyonic forces. See further Ryder 2000; Buckler 2000, pp. 142–144. Soon after, Philip seized Elatea, on the route from Thermopylae to Thebes, which caused panic in Athens (Dem. 18.169–178).

[34] This was the Athenian response to any threat from Philip or news of movements on his part, but it was always a short-term measure and thus amounted to nothing (cf. the criticisms in Dem. 3.4–5). The *eisphora* was an extraordinary tax levied in times of emergency and usually paid by the wealthy; cf. *Prologue* 41.2.

[35] Cf. the criticisms at Dem. 3.5 on how quick the Athenians were to abandon a plan if they believed the threat from Philip was over.

Philip was in the Hellespont,[36] and again when the pirate triremes arrived at Marathon.[37]

[3] Gentlemen of Athens, you are accustomed to deliberate in the same way as someone would rightly deploy a military force—with speed. However, you ought to deliberate leisurely[38] but execute your decisions with zeal. You should reflect that unless you provide for an adequate supply line and put a sensible general in charge of the war, and are willing to stay true to the decisions you make, only your decrees will be left: you will have frittered away all your expenditures, the present situation will be no better, and in a fit of anger you will put whomever you please on trial. I myself would prefer to see you confront your enemies before you try your fellow citizens, for it is not right for us to make war on ourselves rather than on them.

[4] In order that I will not simply criticize[39]—which is the easiest course of all—I will explain how I think you can do this. I ask you not to make noise, and do not think I am just wasting time or introducing delays. For those who say "at once" and "today" are not addressing the point most directly, for we could not prevent what has already happened by sending help today. Instead, it is those who show what force we can provide who will be able to stand fast until we either defeat our enemies or end the war with a settlement. In this way we should no longer suffer badly in the future.

---

[36] It is hard to pinpoint a context for this action in the Hellespont. Clavaud in the Budé text suggests that this is an allusion to Philip's siege of Heraion Teichos, a fortress close to Perinthus, in 352. His action caused the Athenians to vote to deploy forty triremes manned by men over the age of forty-five and to levy a special tax of sixty talents (Dem. 3.4–5) in order to maintain the reestablishment of their influence in the Chersonese. They abandoned this mission, but then some time later, when they heard that Philip was either dead or ill (Dem. 1.13; cf. 3.5, 4.10–11), they sent out a different force to the region.

[37] In May 352 the *Paralus,* one of two state triremes used for religious and other special purposes (Thuc. 8.73–74; Aes. 3.162), made its annual journey to Apollo's sanctuary on Delos (*Ath. Pol.* 56). It stopped at Marathon to offer a sacrifice at the sanctuary of Apollo there, and was captured by Philip (cf. Dem. 4.34).

[38] A reference to the probable rushed nature by which the Assembly dealt with its business and the insufficient time to consider important proposals in much detail; hence, hasty decisions were made: see the Introduction to *Prologues.*

[39] The conclusion to the prologue is very similar to Dem. 4.14–15 (of 351).

22

[1] I think that all of you would agree, gentlemen of Athens, that our city must have the same regard for its own best interests as it does for justice when we deliberate about any of its own affairs, but when we deliberate on behalf of our allies or the Greeks as a whole, as is the case now, it should consider nothing more important than justice.[40] For in the former scenario, it is enough to gain some advantage, but the latter ought also to result in honor. [2] Actions are judged by those who are affected by them, but no one, no matter how powerful, can control what is said about them, but whatever opinion is held about the actions, the people proclaim the same about the actors. Therefore, you must be careful and diligent so that your actions appear just. [3] Everyone should have the same attitude about those who are wronged as he would expect from others towards himself if something were to happen, which I pray will not. However, since certain persons take the opposite view, contrary to their own judgment, I will say a few words to them, and then advise what measures I take to be best for you.

23

[1] Gentlemen of Athens, I do not think that you would consider the damage trifling if an unfavorable and undeserved opinion of our city should arise among the majority of people. Your attitude in this is right, but your actions are not in accord, for you are repeatedly misled into doing things that not even you yourselves hold honorable. I know that all men are happier to hear speakers praise them than rebuke them, yet in pursuing this goodwill I do not think it right to say anything contrary to what I believe is to your advantage.

[2] If you had decided things properly at the start, it would not be necessary to take public action that in private you detest in order to

---

[40] The private interests affected only the Athenians, whereas justice affected the Greeks as a whole. The reference to the allies would be to the Second Athenian Naval Confederacy (see *Prologue* 2.3); there is no mention of any military threat or of warfare in this *Prologue*, so it could come from a speech discussing Athenian hegemony of the confederacy.

prevent what is taking place now from arising. Everyone walks around and says, "How shameful and terrible," and "How long will things like this go on?"—but every man sitting here with you is himself one of those who does such things. Just as I know that it is in your interest to hear the speaker who proposes the best policy, I wish I also knew that it would be in the interest of the speaker who gives the best advice, for I would be much happier. Now, I am afraid. But still, I will not refrain from voicing what I am convinced will prove best, even if you are not so persuaded.[41]

24

[1] Even if someone had never said another word here before, gentlemen of Athens, I think that he would justly meet with sympathy from all of you if he now spoke about the false charges that the ambassadors bring against the city.[42]

In certain other matters, to be beaten by your opponents may not appear disgraceful so much as bad luck, for luck, the people in charge, and many other factors play a role in winning or losing a contest. But when men cannot defend themselves justly to the extent that circumstances allow, we will find that the shame attaches to the intelligence of those who are suffering this. [2] Therefore, if the audience for the speeches about you was a foreign one, I do not think speakers would lie so easily, nor would the listeners put up with much of what they said. But in fact, I think that in general all men take advantage of your good nature, and these men especially have done so now, for I am sure

---

[41] This is similar to the epilogue of Dem. 4 (51).

[42] See also the accusations of ambassadors in *Prologue* 46, and cf. *Prologue* 37 (exiled democrats from Mytilene appealing for help). The ambassadors came from Chios, Byzantium, and Rhodes, cities that were responsible for the Social War (see *Prologue* 2.3). Dem. 15.3 tells us that the Athenians were accused of plotting against these three states, which led to their defection. After the war ended, the democratic government on Rhodes was overturned in favor of an oligarchy supported by Mausolus, satrap of Caria, and in 351 the exiled Rhodian democrats appealed for help to Athens. Not surprisingly, the Athenians gave them short shrift, despite a speech by Demosthenes in the same year urging reconciliation (15, *For the Liberty of the Rhodians*): see further Badian 2000, pp. 31–33; Usher 1999, pp. 213–215.

that they have found that you listen to them against your own interests as no other people would.

[3] Gentlemen of Athens, I think that because of this you should give thanks to the gods and hate these men.[43] For I consider it fortunate for the city that they see you being supplicated by the democrats of Rhodes, who at one time uttered much more contemptuous words against you than these men do.[44] It should rightly make you extremely angry that these ignorant men should not understand this, although it is clear to see, or forget that you have saved each and every one of them many times, and that you have had more inconvenience fixing the results of their recklessness and misfortune, whenever they went to war on their own, than in administering your own affairs. [4] Perhaps it is their fate never to be wise when prosperous,[45] but because of who we are and the city's past actions, it is fitting that we make an effort to show all men that as far as the past, present, and future go, we choose to practice justice, whereas certain others, who want to enslave their fellow citizens, slander them to us.

25

[1] If you, gentlemen of Athens, had the same attitude listening to the speeches of your advisers and judging the results, then offering advice would be the safest course of all. For when the result was fortunate or otherwise (a speaker should always phrase words in the best way), the responsibility would be both yours and the proposer's. Instead, you greatly enjoy listening to those who say what you want, yet you often accuse them of deceiving you if everything does not turn out as you wish. [2] You do not consider that, in looking for and assessing what is best, as far as is humanly possible, and explaining it to you, each man controls his own performance, but the greatest part of the execution and success of these is in the hands of Fortune. It is enough for a mere human to be responsible for his own decisions, but

---

[43] That is, the ambassadors.

[44] In other words, Rhodes was Athens' ally before the Social War, then defected, but now seeks its help to put down the oligarchy.

[45] Note a similar expression in Dem. 15.16.

to be responsible for fate is impossible. [3] If someone discovered how to address the masses without danger, it would be crazy to disregard this procedure. However, since the man who speaks his mind about future events is compelled to share in their consequences and the blame attached to them, I think it disgraceful to speak as a loyal citizen but not stand firm if some danger arises from this.[46]

I pray to the gods that what might benefit both the city and me may come into my mind to utter and into yours to adopt.[47] For I would say that to seek victory in every manner possible is either madness or greed.

26

[1] Gentlemen of Athens, if only it were true that in your present deliberations in the Assembly and in all the others what seemed best to you actually was best in reality! However, when deliberating on weighty public matters, you must be willing to listen to all your advisers, so it seems to me, considering that it is disgraceful, gentlemen of Athens, to raise an uproar[48] now when certain men wish to propose something, but later you listen gladly to the same men censuring what has been done. [2] For I know, and I think you do too, that those who now say the things that you yourselves want to hear please you best, but if something were to arise contrary to what you now foresee—and let this not happen!—you would think that these men had deceived

---

[46] The speaker refers to the fickleness of the Assembly. Public speaking was a dangerous business given the strict laws regulating speakers and officials: Dem. 20.100 and 135 talks of the law inflicting death on the person who was found guilty of deceiving the Assembly, the Boule, and the lawcourts. Cf. *Ath. Pol.* 43.4, 45.2 (with Rhodes 1981, *ad loc.*); Dem. 18.249–250, 322, 23.97; Dem. *Letter* 3.3; Hyp. 5.28–29. See also *Prologues* 6, 29.3, 37.2, 40.

[47] Introductory prayers were common and were sometimes seen as vital to the success of proposals in deliberative speeches; cf. Dem. 3.18: "The speaker is not to blame for that—unless he leaves out the necessary prayers." See also *Prologues* 31, 50.1.

[48] The Athenian Assembly was a noisy place, for often several thousand people attended, and at times (as in the lawcourts), speakers would deliberately raise uproar (*thorubos*) among their audience so as to support their arguments. See further Bers 1985.

you, and those whom you cannot tolerate now will then seem to say what is right. Those who have best managed to persuade you about what you are now considering will benefit the most by their opponents having the chance to speak. [3] For if they are able to show that these men's proposals are not the best, when no blunder has yet been made, then this will free them from danger.[49] But if they cannot do this, they will later have no cause to find fault, for having obtained everything men are obliged to give, a hearing, they will rightly be happy if they are defeated, and with all the rest they will share in the outcome, whatever it may be.[50]

27

[1] When deliberating about such weighty matters,[51] gentlemen of Athens, I think you must grant each of your advisers the freedom to speak. I have never thought that instructing you as to the best policy was hard (to speak simply, I think that you all know the situation) but rather persuading you to do it. For when a measure has been approved and voted in, it is still as far from being enacted as before it was approved. [2] One thing for which I consider you owe thanks to the gods is that those men who not long ago waged war on you because of their own insolence now place the hopes for their own safety in your hands alone. So you are right to be pleased about the present situation.[52] For if you decide as you must about it, the result will be that the slanders put out by those who disparage our city will in fact be eliminated, and our good reputation will remain intact.

28

[1] Gentlemen of Athens, previous speakers roused great and glorious hopes, but I think that most of you have heard them without serious consideration. I have never thought to tell you something for the

---

[49] That is, the Assembly will not censure them: cf. *Prologue* 25.3.

[50] Cf. the similarity with the epilogue to Dem. 14 (30).

[51] This prologue is similar to that of Dem. 15 of 351 (1–2).

[52] Probably a reference to the plea of the exiled Rhodian democrats in 351: see *Prologue* 24 with notes.

sake of quick gratification that I did not think would benefit you afterwards. Of course, it is a characteristic of most men to like those who join
in praising them for whatever they do, and to feel animosity towards
those who are critical. Nevertheless, the sensible man must always try
to ensure that reason is stronger than his desires. [2] I would be pleased
to see you happy at adopting measures that would be beneficial to you,
in order that I might be seen as both pleasing you and making useful
proposals. But since I see you undertaking just the opposite, I think I
must speak against this, even if I will incur the enmity of some. If you
will not face hearing even a single word, it will seem that you are choosing this course not because of a mistake in judgment but because you
naturally want to do wrong. If you listen, perhaps you may be persuaded to change your mind, which I think would most benefit you. If
not, some will say you are ignorant over what is best for you, and others, well, whatever someone wants to say, he will say it.

29

[1] First, it is not new that there are some among you, gentlemen
of Athens, who, when something must be done, will oppose what you
decided.[53] If they did this after you had let them speak during your
earlier deliberations, it would be right to censure them if they insisted
on speaking again for the proposals that had been defeated. There is
nothing astonishing if today they want to speak about things which
at that time you would not listen to, [2] and someone might rightly
blame you, gentlemen of Athens, because whenever you deliberate
about something, you do not allow each man to say what is on his
mind, but if some speakers win you over, you would not listen to the
others. The result is an unpleasant situation for you since those whose
proposals might have persuaded you before you went wrong, you later

---

[53] The Assembly could vote to reopen discussion on any previous business,
and sometimes votes could be revised. An example of this was in 427, when the
Athenians debated the punishment to be inflicted on Mytilene on Lesbos, which
had revolted in the previous year. The Assembly decreed to kill all the men and
to enslave the woman and children, but the next day the people debated the issue
again and revised their decree, voting to kill only the ringleaders of the revolt: see
Thuc. 3.36 – 49.

praise for censuring you. [**3**] I think that this is about to happen again, unless right now you give an impartial hearing to all; put up with this annoyance and choose the best policy, and then treat as worthless those who denounce this policy in any way.

I have thought it right to begin my own speech by telling you what I think about the matter under consideration in order that if this pleases you I may tell you the rest; but if not, then I will not trouble you further nor wear myself out.

30

[**1**] You ought, gentlemen of Athens, to have considered what preparations should be made for the forthcoming campaigns before declaring the war. If the war was not foreseen, then, during your first deliberation about it after war was evident, you should have also considered the preparations for it. If you will say that you have deployed many forces that your commanders have destroyed, no one will accept this from you.[54] For the same people cannot acquit those in charge of their affairs and say that the operations are going badly because of them.[55] [**2**] Since, however, past events cannot be reversed, and we must protect our affairs with our present resources, this is not the time for recriminations, and I will try to offer what I think is the best advice.

First, you must decide on this: each man must display in his actions the same excess of zeal and thirst for victory as the extent of his negligence in previous times, for there is a slim chance that although far behind, we may be able with difficulty to recoup what has been lost. [**3**] Next, we must not be downhearted by what has happened, for the worst aspect of the past happens to be the best for the future.[56] What

---

[54] A possible reference to the Athenian attempts to save Olynthus, when besieged by Philip II, in 348. Despite Demosthenes' three *Olynthiac* speeches, an Athenian fleet arrived too late to save the city. The citizens were either enslaved or fled into exile (Diodorus Siculus 16.53.3). See further Hammond and Griffith 1979, pp. 321–328. The destruction of Olynthus was a popular subject among the orators.

[55] The Assembly would charge a general with a specific directive and then could be swayed by opponents' speeches to take a contrary view.

[56] A proverbial expression found as far back as in Homer, *Iliad* 18.112, and used by Demosthenes in 3.6, 18.192.

do I mean, gentlemen of Athens? That your affairs are in a bad way because you are not doing what you should do, since if you were doing everything that was needed and this was still the situation, then there would be no hope of improvement.[57]

31

[1] Gentlemen of Athens, there is nothing more heinous than public speakers who display the same habits that they censure in others. For no one is so stupid as to say that it does not harm our interests when speakers quarrel among themselves and accuse each other when no one is on trial.[58] I myself think that these men would do best if, when speaking in public, they switched their rivalry with each other to the enemies of the city. And I advise you not to side with either type or to consider how to make either dominant but how all of you will conquer your enemies. [2] I pray to the gods[59] that those who, from rivalry, or spite, or any other motive, say anything other than what they think is in your best interest, stop doing so. For an adviser to offer up a curse is perhaps unusual. Therefore, gentlemen of Athens, I myself blame no one for our sorry state of affairs except all of them together. I think you must make them render an account when you have the leisure time, but for now, you must consider how the present situation might be improved.

32

[1] I wish, gentlemen of Athens, that some of the speakers showed the same zeal for voicing the best advice as they do for their reputation as speakers; if they did, then they would be considered honest rather than clever speakers, and your affairs, as is fitting, would be better. But instead, I think that some are very pleased with their reputation as speakers and show no concern for how the consequences affect you. [2] And indeed I wonder whether speeches such as these are able to

---

[57] Similar lines of argument are found in Dem. 4.2, 9.5.

[58] On the Assembly convened as a court, see *Prologue* 11n25.

[59] On the prayer in the prologue of deliberative speeches, see *Prologues* 25.3, 50.1.

deceive the speaker in the same way as their audience, or whether these men knowingly give advice contrary to what seems to them to be best. For if they do not know that the man who will do what needs to be done does not need courage that comes from words but strength that comes from preparations, and must be confident not because his enemies lack power, but because he will succeed even if they are strong, then the elegance of their speeches, so it seems, has prevented them from understanding what is most important. And if they would not admit their ignorance of this, but give another excuse why they choose their present course, then how can we not see this excuse as worthless, whatever it is?

[3] I will not be turned from speaking what I have in mind, although I see you have been put under a spell, for it would be foolish, since you have wrongly been bewitched by a speech, for the man who intends to give better and more advantageous advice to be afraid. I ask you to listen patiently. Bear in mind that you would not have the views that you hold now unless you had listened to the speeches that persuaded you. [4] Therefore, just as if you were judging a coin to assess its worth, you would think it necessary to test it, so I ask you to examine the speech that has been made in view of what we have to say against it. If you find it beneficial, be persuaded, and good luck to you. However, if, after considering each point, it appears otherwise, then change your minds before you make a mistake and adopt the right course of action.

33

[1] I would like most of all, gentlemen of Athens, for you to be persuaded by what I am about to say; but if it turns out otherwise, then I should be content above all else that I was the one who said it.

The difficulty, so it seems, is not just to tell you what must be done, but also to discover it by one's own investigation. Anyone would understand this if he thought that you would examine not his speech but the troubles that you are facing, and attach more importance to being seen as an honest man than as a clever speaker. [2] At any rate (and let some good fortune come to me), when it occurred to me to consider the present situation, I happened to think of many expressions which you would have listened to with pleasure. For on the topic of your being the most just of the Greeks, I saw and I see that there was much to be said, or how you are descended from the best ancestors, and many such themes. These lines give pleasure when they are spoken but afterwards fade to nothing. [3] The speaker must show himself an adviser for a particular course of action by which you afterwards gain a real good benefit.[60] I already know from experience that this is rare and hard to discover. For it is not enough for someone to visualize such policies unless he can persuade you to share in their implementation. Nevertheless, it is my job, I think, to tell you what I am convinced is in your best interests; your job is to listen and decide and, if it pleases you, adopt the policy.

34

[1] It is clear, gentlemen of Athens, that when you recently thought that you did not need to listen to those who wanted to speak against what so-and-so said,[61] what is now taking place would occur, namely, that those who were prevented then would speak at another Assembly. Therefore, if you do the same as before and refuse to hear those who wish to speak in favor of what was adopted then, these men will again take the matter back to another Assembly and denounce these things. [2] In no way, gentlemen of Athens, could the present situation be made worse, nor could you appear more foolish than if none of the decisions you made are carried out to the end, or if you disregard your best interests and make no headway towards improvement, and like a theatrical audience you side with those who perform first. No, gentlemen of Athens, you must perform this onerous task and be ready to listen to both sides equally. Then you must first choose a policy you will actually follow, then treat anyone who speaks against what you have decided in this way as a criminal and ill disposed to you. [3] It is understandable that someone who was not allowed to speak would be convinced that his policy is better than what was decided by you, but after you have heard his proposal and given your vote, if he continues

---

[60] There is a similar expression in Dem. 8.73.

[61] The Greek phrase *ho deina* ("so-and-so" or "a certain speaker") is deliberately vague to avoid naming opponents, which was considered inappropriate etiquette in an Assembly: Worthington 2004b, p. 142. See also *Prologue* 45.1.

to act shamelessly and refuses to agree with the opinion of the majority, it will appear that he has some other motive that is not just. I thought that I should stay quiet on this occasion, if I saw you holding true to what was decided, for I am one of those who are convinced that this is in your best interest; yet some men seem to have changed their minds thanks to these men's speeches. Perhaps you know that what they say is neither true nor beneficial to you, but I will instruct you in case you happen to be ignorant.

35

[1] Gentlemen of Athens, the right course was that each man should have persuaded you to do what he thought best at the time when you were first deliberating on these matters, in order to avoid the two most destructive outcomes for the city, namely, that none of your decisions should be final and that by changing your minds you should convict yourselves of lunacy. Since some men who then kept quiet are now being critical, I want to say a few things to them.

[2] I am astonished at how these men conduct politics, and I think it foul. For if they could have presented their views when you were deliberating, but instead chose to criticize after the decisions were made, they do the job of sycophants[62] not, so they claim, of loyal citizens. I would be pleased to ask them (and I hope what I intend to say will not be the start of any quarrel) why, in praising the Spartans in other respects, they do not emulate what is the most admirable of their customs but rather they do the opposite of this? [3] For they say, gentlemen of Athens, that among them each man can utter any thought he has until the time to vote, but when the decision has been ratified they all approve and work together, even those who opposed the decision.[63] Therefore, even though they are few, they triumph over many, and

---

[62] As litigation increased in Athens so too did the number of sycophants, who accused all and sundry in return for monetary gain; see further the Series Introduction.

[63] The speaker refers to the Apella, the Spartan Assembly. Originally, discussion was not allowed (Plut., *Lycurgus* 6). Instead, a proposal was put to the people who voted for or against it by shouting, and the loudest shout decided the issue. Later, however, discussion did take place, for Thuc. 1 describes several lively debates in Sparta that led to the Peloponnesian War.

through opportunities they acquire what they cannot take in war, and no means of securing some advantage for themselves escapes them. Not like us, by Zeus,[64] who, because of these men and those like them, working to outdo one another and not the enemy,[65] have squandered all our time. [4] If someone makes peace in wartime, we hate him; and if someone talks of war in peacetime, we fight him; and if someone advises us to be quiet and mind our own business, we claim that he is speaking wrongly; and overall we are full of accusations and empty hopes.

What do you suggest, someone might ask, since you criticize this? By Zeus, I will tell you.

36

[1] First of all, gentlemen of Athens, it does not seem entirely reasonable to me that someone would fear that your deliberations would be poorer because you do not want to listen to those advising you. In the first place, Fortune arranges many of your affairs automatically and does a good job, as you would pray for, because few things would turn out as well if left to the foresight of those in charge. Next, you know beforehand not only the words that each man will utter but also the reasons why each of them speaks, and, although not malicious, I would have added for what fee. [2] You seem to me wise to cut back the time for being cheated to a minimum. If I wanted to say the same thing as the others, I should not have thought it necessary to disturb you by speaking. But now I think I have something to say that will be in your best interests to hear, and completely different from what is expected by the majority. It will take only a short time. When you have heard it, consider it, and, if it pleases you, adopt it.

37

[1] Gentlemen of Athens, I will make the start of my speech short and just, and I will not even say everything. For I believe that whoever wants to deceive you looks for a way with his words to conceal from

---

[64] An oath was a common rhetorical trick in order to emphasize and to lend a sense of piety to an argument. See also *Prologues* 45.1, 46.3, 48.2.

[65] There is some similarity here with Dem. 2.25.

you, the audience, unpleasant aspects of the situation, but someone who has decided to deal with you plainly will first say which party he has stepped forward to support, [2] in order that if, after hearing this, you are willing to listen to the words that follow, he may explain and reveal the proposals that seem best to him, whereas if you reject him, he would leave and neither annoy you nor wear himself out.[66]

So I will say this first. It seems to me that the people of Mytilene have been wronged, and it is only right that you exact justice for them.[67] I can tell you how you can exact it after I have shown that they have been wronged and that it is right for you to help them.

38

[1] In the first place, it is not such a surprise, gentlemen of Athens, that it is hard for those who want to advise you to have trouble finding the words. For when the situation under consideration is bad, advice concerning it must necessarily be unpleasant. Therefore, if there is the hope that the situation will improve if you refuse to listen, then you must do this. However, if everything will become worse not better from this, why must you allow things to reach rock bottom, and only then try to save the situation that is worse than now and more difficult to manage, when it is possible even now in our present condition to put things right and improve the situation?

[2] Naturally, you feel angry about these misfortunes, but it is not reasonable or right to be angry at everyone in turn rather than those who are responsible. For those who are not responsible for what happened in the past and have some advice how the future may be better rightly deserve your thanks, not your enmity. If you get angry with them inappropriately, you will make them hesitant to stand up to speak. [3] I am aware that it is often not those responsible who suffer

---

[66] See *Prologues* 6, 25.3, 29.3.

[67] At the end of the Social War in 355 (see *Prologue* 2.3) Mytilene, principal city on the island of Lesbos, suffered an oligarchy; the *Prologue* suggests that the exiled democrats were appealing for assistance to restore democracy in much the same way as had the exiled Rhodian democrats (see *Prologues* 24 and 46). Support was not given (Dem. 13.8, 15.19–20; both passages admonish the Athenians as part of a general proclamation of the superiority of democracy over oligarchy).

something unpleasant but those who get in the way of angry people. Nevertheless, I stand up to advise you, for I trust, gentlemen of Athens, that you will not find me responsible for past problems, and that I have better advice for you than the others.

39

[1] Gentlemen of Athens, the events that have taken place are such as you have heard, but you must not be dismayed, since to lose heart will not help the present situation and would be unworthy of you, but if you think how you can correct the situation, then this would appear proper and worthy of your reputation. Men such as you say you are must show themselves superior to others in times of hardship. [2] I would not in any way have wanted these disasters to afflict the city or you to endure bad luck. But if this was going to happen and divine will has reserved it for us, then I think that it is to your benefit that the events happened as they did. For Fortune brings about sharp changes and these affect both sides equally, but what happens because of men's cowardice makes defeat inevitable. [3] I think even the victors are aware that if you have the will and are aroused by what happened, then it is not yet entirely clear whether what has happened is good fortune or the opposite for them. And if it transpires that the event emboldens them, this would also be to your advantage, for the more they despise you, the sooner they will make a mistake.

40

[1] I do not think, gentlemen of Athens, that you are now deliberating only about the city you have in mind but about all the allied cities.[68] For whatever you decide about this city, the others are naturally watching you and expect to obtain the same treatment for themselves. Consequently, you must work hard for what is best as well as for your own reputation so that it will be clear that you are deliberating about both expediency and justice.

---

[68] Perhaps the allied cities in the Second Athenian Naval Confederacy: see *Prologue* 2.3.

[2] The start of all such affairs lies with the generals, and most of those who sail from your ports do not think that they need to cultivate your friends, when they have inherited and always shared the same dangers as you. Instead, each one has secured his own private friends, and now expects you to accept those who flatter them as your friends. But the situation is just the opposite.[69] [3] For you would find no enemies more adversarial or more entrenched than these, for the more they profit by cheating you, the more they think they will be punished for their crimes. No one would have goodwill towards those whom he expects will harm him. Perhaps the present occasion is not the time to accuse them, but I will advise you as to what I think is beneficial to you.

41

[1] Gentlemen of Athens, I think that not one of you is so ill disposed to the city as not to be troubled and pained by the events. If it were possible to undo any of these events by getting upset, I would be advising you all to do this. But since the situation cannot be otherwise, and you must think how you might not suffer the same thing in the future, just as you are angry over what has happened, gentlemen of Athens, so you must strive hard to prevent the same thing from happening again. And do not think that any of your advisers has a plan that can rescue us from our present predicament without any sharing in the burden. For no speech could do that, but only some god.

[2] The root of the present situation lies in this, that some speakers have, for the sake of earning your favor at the moment, claimed that it was not necessary to pay a special tax[70] or do war service, but that everything would happen on its own. These misconceptions should have been refuted by some other speaker, relying on the sort of reputation that benefits the city, but it seems to me that in some ways Fortune is now kinder to you than your leaders. [3] For each loss you incur is a sign of the depravity of our leaders, and the fact that everything was lost not long ago I judge to be a benefit of your good fortune. Meanwhile, while Fortune gives you a breathing space and holds back your enemies,

---

[69] On attitudes to corrupt officials, see *Prologues* 6, 25.3, 29.3, 37.2.

[70] For the *eisphora*, see *Prologue* 21.2n34.

take care about the future. Otherwise, consider how you can prevent yourselves from judging those appointed to each of the commands at the same time, while your situation, gentlemen of Athens, declines. For it is impossible that this will endure without some great miracle, if no one pitches in to help it.[71]

42

[1] Gentlemen of Athens, it is not unreasonable that those who consistently plead on behalf of oligarchies should be convicted of doing this now. But someone would have more reason to be amazed by the fact that you who know this often listen with more pleasure to these men than to those who speak on your behalf. Perhaps it is hard to do everything correctly in public affairs, just as it is in private ones, but we should not overlook the most important matters. [2] All other considerations are of less weight, but when you listen lightheartedly to speeches on behalf of constitutional matters and murders and the subversion of democracy,[72] how can you not think that you are out of your minds? For all other men learn from the examples of others and become more cautious themselves,[73] but you are unable to be afraid even when you hear of the misfortunes of others. Instead, though in private you think that waiting for the inevitable is foolish, in public you seem to me to be waiting for just this, and you will know it when you suffer.

43

[1] Perhaps none of you has ever inquired, gentlemen of Athens, why it is that men who fare badly deliberate better about matters than those who fare well. This happens for no other reason than that the latter fear nothing and do not think that the dangers someone might predict could affect them, whereas those who are close to their mistakes, after reaching their sorry state, become wise and moderate about the

---

[71] There is similarity here with Dem. 3.35–36.

[72] That is, speeches advocating oligarchy over democracy; on the Athenians' fear of oligarchy, cf. *Prologue* 2.

[73] The passage is similar to Dem. 15.16.

future. [2] Serious men, therefore, should show more zeal for moderation when their present fortune is not favorable. For no danger is so terrible that those on their guard cannot guard against it,[74] but those who belittle it may expect to suffer it. I say this not in order that I might frighten you unduly but so that you do not, because of your present prosperity, scorn the dangers that would beset you if you do not anticipate your affairs, but rather take care to avoid them without suffering, as becomes those who claim they are exceeded by no one in wisdom.

44

[1] I assume that the time for pleasing you and the time for putting forward the proposals that I think best are not the same, gentlemen of Athens. For I see that often pleasing you by contradicting my personal opinion brings more enmity than if I opposed you from the start. Therefore, if all of you felt the same way, I would not have come forward if you seemed to me to be choosing what needed to be done, for I think it is redundant to speak to those who are doing what is necessary on their own, nor again if the opposite applied. For I would have thought that a single individual like myself would be more likely not to know what is best than all of you. [2] However, since I see that some of you have the same view as I do but the opposite to that of others, I will attempt with these men to persuade the others. If you think you do not need to agree to listen, then you will be wrong. But if you listen in silence to the end, then you will gain an advantage, either because you will be persuaded, if we seem to suggest something beneficial, or because you will be more firmly convinced that your own view is right. For if the ways in which we think you are wrong appear worthless, you will have proof for choosing the views you now hold.

45

[1] I wish, gentlemen of Athens, that a certain speaker[75] who has gained some fame for speaking to you about his proposals had won equal praise for putting them into practice. For I am not ill disposed to

---

[74] There is a similar passage at Dem. 1.3.

[75] See *Prologue* 34.1.

this man, by the gods,[76] and I wish you would enjoy some benefit. However, beware, gentlemen of Athens, for making a good speech and choosing beneficial policies are very different: for one is the task of an orator and the other of a man with good sense. [2] So now you, the majority, and especially the oldest of you, are not expected to be able to speak like the cleverest orators, for this ability comes from practice. However, you are expected to have as much good sense as, and even more than, them, for it is a wide range of experience that empowers us with this. Therefore, gentlemen of Athens, do not show that at the present time you are unaware that the courageous and brave acts related in speeches are a pleasure to hear but are dangerous in deed unless accompanied by adequate preparations and force. [3] For example, see what a fine saying this is, not to give a free hand to those who do wrong. However, first look hard at the deed itself. Those who want to realize the glory of this saying in action must defeat the enemy in battle. For, gentlemen of Athens, all things are easy to say but not all things are easy to achieve, for there is not as much work and sweat before speaking as before acting. [4] I do not believe that in natural ability you are inferior to the Thebans (I would be mad to think so), but are not so well prepared.[77] I say that you must now start making preparations since you have thus far neglected these, but not begin the actual struggle. Thus, I am not criticizing the whole plan, but I am opposed to the manner of putting it into practice.

46

[1] Gentlemen of Athens, you have all seen the zeal with which the ambassadors[78] denounced our city. Apart from some complaint (I do not remember what) they tried to lay everything else on you. If their

---

[76] On the oath, see *Prologues* 35.3, 46.3, 48.2.

[77] The reference to Thebes and to a proposal to do battle suggests that a possible context is the alliance with Thebes against Philip, which Demosthenes secured in 339 (cf. Dem. 18.153): see the Introduction. This prologue cannot postdate 335 since in that year Alexander the Great razed Thebes to the ground: see the Introduction.

[78] These, presumably, were the Chians, Byzantines, and Rhodians, who have appeared elsewhere: see *Prologue* 24.1; cf. 27.2. However, the speaker's reaction to them is much more harsh here than in the other prologues.

allegations were true, you would have reason to be thankful that they were thus denouncing us to our faces and not to others. [2] However, since in their speeches they warped the truth and omitted some matters that would rightly bring you great praise, and made false charges that do not apply to you, you can with justice consider them dishonest when these actions have been proved. If they chose to appear to be clever orators rather than to be thought true, upstanding men, not even they themselves, so it seems, would claim to be honorable men. [3] It is just as difficult to stand up and speak before you on your behalf as it is easy to speak against you. For, by Athena,[79] I do not think any other men would listen when reminded of faults that are really theirs as you do when you listen to accusations of faults that are not yours. Moreover, I do not believe that these men would lie so boldly if they did not know this and if it was not clear that you more than anyone are ready to hear whatever someone may say against you.

[4] If you must be punished for your naïveté, it would be this: to listen to speeches attacking the city without justification. However, if something must justly be said on behalf of the truth, then I have come forward for this purpose, not in the belief that I will be able to speak worthily of your past actions [5] but that I can make it clear that these actions, whatever someone may say about them, were just. I wish, gentlemen of Athens, that you would become equally intent listeners on your own behalf and not be duped into competing to praise the speeches of these men. For no one would still ascribe the crime to you if some clever speaker deceived you but to those who worked hard for the purpose of deceiving you.

47

[1] I think that all of you, gentlemen of Athens, would say that you want to have those measures adopted which each of you considers best for the city. But it happens that the same criteria are not used by everyone for judging the best. Otherwise, some of you would not be asking me to speak and others not to speak. Now, it is not necessary to say anything to those who believe that the same proposals are

---

[79] On oaths in speeches, see *Prologues* 35.3, 45.1, 48.2.

advantageous as the man intending to speak, for they are already persuaded, but I want to speak briefly to those who consider that the opposite course is beneficial. [2] If they are not willing to listen, then obviously they cannot learn a single thing, any more than if they listen quietly when no one else is speaking. However, if they do listen, then they cannot fail to gain one of two good benefits: either all of you will be persuaded and have the same opinion, so you can decide unanimously—and nothing better than this could happen as far as the present situation is concerned—, or, if the speaker is unable to enlighten you, you will have a greater confidence in what you have decided. [3] Apart from these, there has arisen an invidious suspicion that although you came to the Assembly thinking it necessary to choose the best plan from what would be proposed, it is clear that you were convinced of something in your own minds before making a decision based on the speeches—so firmly convinced, in fact, that you are not willing to hear anything said against it.

48

[1] Perhaps I seem to some of you, gentlemen of Athens, to be a troublemaker, always speaking about the same things again and again. However, if you consider matters correctly, it will be clear that it is not right to hold me responsible for this, but rather those who disobey your decrees. For if at the start those men had done what you decreed, it would have been unnecessary for us to speak a second time, nor again if they had obeyed after the second time.⁸⁰ But as it is, the more often you vote for appropriate measures, the less they seem to me to be ready to do it. [2] Previously, by the gods, I did not know the meaning of this saying, "The office reveals the man";⁸¹ now, I think I could explain it to others. For the officials, or some of them—not to blame them all—, give not the slightest thought to your decrees but to how they will profit. If I could have made a payment, someone would rightly criticize

---

⁸⁰ Not a reference to the Assembly's reopening previous matters of debate but, as is revealed towards the prologue's end, to certain men who fail to comply with state directives on the assessment of liturgies (on which, see *Prologue* 14.2).

⁸¹ This expression is taken up by Demosthenes at 19.247 to denounce Aeschines when he quoted from Sophocles' *Antigone* 175–190.

me if I chose to trouble you over a trifling expense. However, in fact, I cannot, as even these men know. [3] If they think I am going to give them money for the liturgies⁸² they have to perform for you, they talk nonsense. Perhaps they want this and expect it. Well, I will not do it. If they contribute, I will launch the ship and perform my duty; if not, then I will reveal to you those who are responsible.⁸³

49

[1] I do not consider that any sensible man would disagree, gentlemen of Athens, that it would be best of all for the city from the outset not to do anything against its own interest, but if it does, those who will oppose should be present straightaway. However, we must add the condition that you are willing to listen and learn, for it is no good for a speaker to speak the best policy unless he has an audience. [2] It would also be profitable, as a second measure, if someone deceives you by a special opportunity or because of the time of the day or some other cause, that there be someone acting as reexaminer when you are willing to listen for your own good, in order that if what you passed proves to be what those who proposed it said at the time, you may put it into practice more confidently, for it has been tested, but if it is found to be different, you may stop it before proceeding further. For it would be terrible if, when people erred over the best policy, they had to adopt the worst and could not reconsider and choose a second time from the speaker's proposals. [3] I see that all other men are always

---

⁸² On liturgies, see *Prologue* 14.2.

⁸³ In the fourth century, trierarchies shared by several wealthy men, rather than the fifth-century practice of individual trierarchies, became normal as a result of greater financial burdens and costs: Jordan 1975, pp. 61–73; cf. pp. 231–232. In 357/6 about 1,200 wealthy men in Athens were grouped into symmories or boards and were responsible for maintaining the triremes ([Dem.] 47.21–23; cf. Dem. 14.16). However, this system proved to be inequitable as some of these men were not as wealthy as others, but all paid the same contribution towards the maintenance of a trireme. The speaker is protesting that despite the legal assessment that the Assembly decided, he is being forced to contribute more than his fair share.

ready to be held accountable whenever they are convinced that one of their proposals has been rightly adopted.[84] But these men, on the contrary, make accusations if you want to reverse a previous error, thinking that their fraud should carry more weight than the test of time. Therefore, the majority of you perhaps are aware of the aggressiveness of these men, but it is every man's duty, when he has been granted the right to speak, to state the policy that he considers best.

50

[1] I pray that every speaker proposes whatever may benefit the whole city, but you may choose the course, gentlemen of Athens.[85] For my part, I will tell you what I am convinced is in your best interests. I ask only this: do not assume that those who urge you to go to war are therefore courageous nor that those who try to oppose them are therefore cowards. For the same test does not apply to words and deeds, gentlemen of Athens; now, we must show that we have deliberated wisely, and then, if we in fact decide on this course, we must show courage. [2] Your fervor deserves the highest praise of all: it is what any loyal citizen would pray for. However, the more zealous it is, the more you need to see that it is put to good use. For choosing a course of action earns no praise unless the result is beneficial and good. I know I once heard one of you, gentlemen of Athens, who seemed to be neither ignorant nor inexperienced in war—I refer to Iphicrates.[86] [3] He said that a general must choose to risk danger "not

---

[84] The passage is very similar to Dem. 19.2.

[85] On introductory prayers, see *Prologue* 25.3n47; cf. 31.

[86] On Iphicrates, one of the great Athenian generals of the fourth century, see, e.g., Demosthenes' praise of him at 21.62–63 and 23.129–131. In 390 Iphicrates defeated a Spartan force and was awarded a public statue in Athens and the state honors of *sitesis* (free meals for life in the Prytaneum or Town Hall) and *proedria* (a reserved front seat at the theater). In 356/5 he sailed with Menestheus (cf. *Letter* 3.31) and Timotheus (cf. *Erotic Essay* 46) to Chares (cf. *Letter* 3.31) as joint commanders of an Athenian fleet during the Social War (see *Prologue* 2.3). They were defeated in battle and tried for accepting bribes. Iphicrates and Menestheus were acquitted, and Iphicrates died in 353.

so that this or that will be the result but just this," those were his words. The meaning is clear: that one must fight nobly. When you march out, whoever leads you is your master, but now each one of you is your own general. You must show that you have adopted measures that in every way will be beneficial for the city, and do not diminish our present prosperity for the sake of mere hopes for the future.

51

I should have thought, gentlemen of Athens, that no one who was confident about his action would complain about those who want to bring them up for discussion. For the more often someone inquires into them, the higher the reputation of those responsible for them. Nevertheless, I think that these men seem to make it clear that they have not acted in the best interests of the city. Surely it is because they will be convicted if they give another accounting of their actions that they try to avoid it and accuse us of acting terribly. And yet when you accuse those who want to investigate you of acting terribly, what shall we say about those who in these very affairs have deceived us?

52

It would be right for you, gentlemen of Athens, to feel the same anger towards those who try to deceive you as towards those who succeed. For they have done whatever was in their power, and they led you along. The reason why their plans have not come to fruition is because of Fortune, and the better understanding you have now than when they cheated you. Nevertheless, I think that the city is so far from punishing these criminals that in view of the tricks and deviousness and certain paid services[87] that you have been subjected to, you should be happy if you can avoid suffering anything bad. The present occasion is not the most fitting for someone to denounce their venality, but I want to say what I consider beneficial in the matter that I stood up to address.

---

[87] Services held by those who received pay for them as opposed to unpaid offices of state or liturgies (which came out of personal wealth) could soon become channels of financial corruption; cf. *Prologue* 55.3.

53

[1] Gentlemen of Athens, the abuse and disorder that habitually damage the city have come from the same men now as always. However, I do not want to criticize these men, for perhaps they do this out of anger or rivalry or, the most important of all, because it is profitable for them to do it. You yourselves are to blame, gentlemen of Athens, if, when you gather to discuss important public affairs, you sit and listen to private abuses and on your own you cannot understand that the slanders that all the speakers level against one other, without there being a trial, mean you will be accountable for anything they prove against one another. [2] Except for a few men, perhaps (I will not say everyone), not one of them slanders another in order to improve any of your affairs—far from it—but in order that he himself may without trouble do the same thing that he called the most heinous crime imaginable when he accused someone else of doing it. [3] Do not take my word for it that this is the case, but consider it for a while. Does anyone ever stand up before you and say, "Gentlemen of Athens, I have come forward because I want to seize something of yours, not to benefit you"? Obviously no one; instead, they give reasons like "on your behalf" and "because of you."

Come now, gentlemen of Athens, consider why is it that when everyone speaks "on your behalf" you are not on the whole better off now than before, but these men who all say "on your behalf" and never said "on my behalf" have gone from rags to riches? They say they love you, gentlemen of Athens; however, they love themselves, not you. [4] They give you the chance to laugh and to applaud and sometimes to hope, but they would not want you to acquire any real benefit for the city. On the day you get rid of your apathy, you will not even be able to stand the sight of them. But for now, gentlemen of Athens, they control the people with a drachma and a *chous*[88] and four obols,[89]

---

[88] The drachma payment was for attending the Assembly (*Ath. Pol.* 62.2). The *chous* was the measure of the grain dole that each citizen received (Dem. 34.37).

[89] If the speaker refers to the daily rate of pay for serving as a juror, there is a problem, for that figure was three obols. Clavaud in the Budé Text puts forward the attractive explanation that the four obols are the theoric payment and draws

giving you sustenance in the same way as doctors treat a sick man. The doctors' diet neither builds your strength nor lets you die, and the politicians' diet neither lets you give it up and get better, nor can it suffice by itself.[90]

54[91]

It is just, gentlemen of Athens, and right and important that, as you normally do, we should observe how our dealings with the gods shall be pious. Therefore, we have performed our duty carefully for you, for we have sacrificed to Zeus the Savior, and to Athena, and to Victory, and these sacrifices have been favorable and auspicious for you. We also sacrificed to Persuasion, and to the Mother of the Gods, and to Apollo,[92] and here also the omens were favorable. And the sacrifices to the other gods also promised protection, stability, prosperity, and safety for you. Therefore, receive the blessings that the gods are giving us.

55

[1] It appears that there was a time, gentlemen of Athens, when the people forced any man whom it regarded as capable and honest to take part in public service and hold political office, not from any lack of those wanting to do this (for while I judge the city fortunate in everything else, I think that it has never had one piece of good luck, that it ran out of people who want to make a profit from public business),

---

attention to Dem. 3.30–31. In this passage, Demosthenes berates the people for the ease by which the politicians control them by doling out all sorts of gratuities, including theoric money. However, from Dem. 18.28, we learn that the theoric payment for a seat in the theater was two obols. On the Theoric Fund, see *Letter* 3.2n50.

[90] There is a similarity with Dem. 3.33.

[91] This text seems to have been included in the prologues erroneously, for it does not appear to be a proper prelude to a speech but an official report by a state-appointed commission to perform certain sacrifices. Those who performed the sacrifices received payment (cf. Dem. 21.171, of Meidias).

[92] When individuals or those acting on behalf of cities went to an oracular site with a particular issue, they asked to which god or gods they should sacrifice in order to secure a favorable resolution, and they were often told to sacrifice to several; see, e.g., Dem. 21.52–53, and cf. Xen., *Anabasis* 3.1.6.

but the people, gentlemen of Athens, made a fine show of this for itself, and it profited the city. [2] For when those men were repeatedly
yoked to others who were serious and just in their private lives, they
proved themselves more cautious in their public lives, while those of
you who were honest and just officials, though not at all competent at
obstruction and partisan politics, were not excluded from the competition for honor. But now, gentlemen of Athens, you appoint magistrates in exactly the same way as priests.[93] Then you are amazed when
this one is thriving and that one continually seizes large sums from
you, and the rest of you walk around envying them their prosperity.
[3] For you are most notorious for taking away the offices that are
yours, and laying down laws about them—if someone serves twice in
the city magistrates[94] or some such thing—but you always let the
same men be generals.[95] There is good reason for those who are in military service to continue, but it is foolish to keep paying others, who
do nothing yet have an unlimited term. You need to bring in some of
your own class, for they are many. If you strike a balance, then anyone
who is worthy will voluntarily come forward soon after.

56

[1] Gentlemen of Athens, it seems to me fine and proper for a man
who has convinced himself that he has something beneficial to say to

---

[93] The majority of the priesthoods were hereditary ([Dem.] 59.104) but some
were appointed by lot ([Dem.] 59.106). In what follows, the speaker shows concern that the upper stratum of society mostly holds public offices and that its
members exploit them and the people. Instead, he wants men from other walks
of life also to stand for public office.

[94] There were ten *astunomoi,* five for Athens and five for the Piraeus, the port
of Athens: *Ath. Pol.* 50.2 with Rhodes 1981, pp. 573–575. They had a number of responsibilities that included monitoring payments to female musicians, building
regulations, and maintaining the general hygiene of the streets. Reelection to office
(excluding the generalship and serving on the Boule) was not permitted by law.

[95] Reelection to the office of general was permitted: *Ath. Pol.* 62.3, with
Rhodes 1981, pp. 696–697. Thus, generals could exploit the office as a political
power base, and some were reelected to the post many times, such as Pericles, who
was general fifteen times (Plut., *Pericles* 16.4) and Phocion who was general a record forty-five times (Plut., *Phocion* 8.1–2).

come forward, but I think it absolutely disgraceful to force those who are not willing to listen to him. And I think that, if you are willing to take my advice today, you will be better able to choose the best policy, and you will make shorter the speeches of those who climb up.[96] [2] What, then, do I advise? First, gentlemen of Athens, ask the man who steps forward to speak only about the issues under consideration. For someone may include many other matters in his speech and make many funny remarks, especially if he is a clever speaker, as some of these men are. If you came just to listen to words, then you should say and hear them; if you came to deliberate about deciding on a course of action, then I urge you to judge the measures in themselves as far as you can, ignoring the rhetorical touches that are intended to deceive. [3] That is the first thing I say. Second, and perhaps this will seem paradoxical in connection with reducing the length of speeches, is that you listen in silence. Not many arguments are possible, unless speakers want to waffle on in vain, in deciding whether this measure or that is beneficial, and which the city might with more justice choose, and no one needs to repeat them. As for the view that it is only right to listen and respond to the reaction of the crowd,[97] and let one speech follow another, no one would be unable to do that. However, you do not get rid of speeches with heckling, for then you are compelled to listen to speeches that have nothing to do with the matter in hand. Therefore, my opinion on the matter that you are debating is this.

---

[96] "Climb up"—that is, onto the *bema* or platform, from which speakers would address the Assembly on the Pnyx; see *Prologue* 6n18.

[97] *Thorubos* (uproar) is the noun here; see *Prologue* 26.1n.

LETTERS 1–6

INTRODUCTION

We have six letters attributed to Demosthenes, of which five (1, 2, 3, 4, and 6) deal with public matters and are addressed to the Council (Boule) and Assembly of Athens, where such letters were commonly read. They give advice on matters affecting the state, and thus are similar to a deliberative speech before the people. The other letter (5) is a private one of complaint to a non-Athenian called Heracleodorus. As is clear from their content, the first, second, third, and fourth letters were written during Demosthenes' exile after his trial in the Harpalus affair (approximately March 323 to perhaps early spring 322), and they have a unifying "theme" of working to effect his recall. For the historical background to the letters, see the Introduction.

It is impossible to date the fifth letter, although the reference in Section 5 to Demosthenes as not one of the foremost statesmen, hence a young man perhaps at the start of his political career, could point to as early as 355. To judge from its context, the sixth letter was sent to the Athenians in the early stages of the Lamian War that broke out after Alexander the Great's death (June 10 or 11, 323) and lasted to August 322 (Demosthenes was recalled several months before it ended).

The authorship of the letters is controversial. Plutarch (*Demosthenes* 26.2), Quintilian (10.1.1–7), and Cicero (*Brutus* 121, *Orator* 15) say that Demosthenes wrote letters, and Plutarch cites an appeal that Demosthenes put forward in the second letter.[1] However, Cicero merely (and

---

[1] "He tells us that he was overcome with shame at these accusations and . . . his weak health made it impossible for him to endure being in prison"; cf. *Letter* 2.17 and *Letter* 3.40.

mistakenly) states that the *Letters* show that Demosthenes was a pupil of Plato (*Brutus* 121, *Orator* 15), while Quintilian has the barest reference to them. Critics and lexicographers of later antiquity accepted the *Letters* as genuine, and extracts from them are often quoted in their works.[2]

The letters may have been forged either by students at rhetorical schools or by Demosthenes' sympathizers after his death, given that they are so different in style from Demosthenes' speeches. However, the rhetorical style of a forensic or a deliberative speech was very different from that of an open letter, which expressed an opinion or took the form of an *apologia* (as do most of Demosthenes' letters). Thus, we ought to expect a different style, a point that Quintilian makes in his comparison of Demosthenes and Cicero. Although Cicero's letters were intended to be read out in the Senate, his forensic speeches are very different in style from them. Therefore, it is no leap of faith to expect the same with Demosthenes' speeches and his letters.

A turning point came with the publication of Jonathan Goldstein's *The Letters of Demosthenes* (1968). Goldstein's careful and detailed historical and stylistic examination of the first four concluded that they were genuine and, further, that they had the common theme of Demosthenes' exoneration and return to Athens (something that would not concern a later forger). Goldstein's arguments are compelling, and the reader is directed to his book for further information, especially for his rhetorical analysis of them and historical commentary on them.

Although there can be no certainty about the authenticity of *Letters* 5 and 6, in his brief discussion of them Goldstein (1968, pp. 261–264) rejects a Demosthenic authorship. If the allusion in *Letter* 5.3 to Demosthenes as a young man is correct, then it cannot have been written by Demosthenes when he was in exile. More important is its unusual praise of Plato's school and erroneous information that Demosthenes

---

[2] Harpocration cited the second letter under the name of "Calauria" (the island in the Saronic Gulf [modern Poros] to which Demosthenes fled) as evidence that it is Demosthenic, and he cited passages from Sections 30 and 38 of the third letter. Hermogenes quoted the opening and some of Section 8 of the second letter and accepted the third as genuine (as did Photius). Goldstein (1968, pp. 4–5) has a convenient summary of the arguments against authenticity.

studied under Plato (5.3). Goldstein suggests that it could have been written as a "collector's item," to make Athens' greatest orator appear to praise Plato's teachings. *Letter 6* is also problematic, but despite Goldstein's reservations, there are grounds for arguing that it was written by Demosthenes shortly before his recall to Athens.[3]

Goldstein (1968) also argued, on chronological grounds, that the order of the first four letters should be 3, 2, 4, 1 (5 and 6, being much shorter and especially since 5 is probably spurious, may as well stay in that order). For the purpose of the present volume, I retain the traditional order.

Demosthenes' *Letters* are all too often neglected, yet they can be read with the same enjoyment as his speeches. We have in the letters a sense of dramatic immediacy, the use of emotion (such as pity, pride, injured indignation), patriotic appeals, the lauding of Athens' system of government and the rule of law, all testimony to Demosthenes' rhetorical prowess.

LETTER I. ON POLITICAL HARMONY

Introduction

Section 13 indicates that this letter was written after Alexander's death in 323 but before the outbreak of the Lamian War soon afterwards. We can imagine that there was fierce debate between the militant Hyperides and the cautious general Phocion, who was against war (Plut., *Phocion* 23.1–2). The richer citizens were also against it not because they were Macedonian sympathizers but because they would be funding the war effort, but they were simply voted down (Diodorus Siculus 18.10). Sections 11–12 indicate that preparations for war were already well in hand, and its final sections encourage the Athenians to make war with the argument that Fortune is finally on their side (see 13n on fortune or *tychē*).

The letter was written when Demosthenes was on the island of Calauria, south of Aegina, from where he could gaze across to the Attic peninsula (cf. *Letter* 2.20). It calls for a general amnesty and

---

[3] Cf. Clavaud in the Budé Text, and now Worthington 2003b.

political harmony in order to end the dissension in Athens.[4] Goldstein (1968, pp. 62, 87) is right, however, to see it as a subtle *apologia* and thus part of the underlying "theme" of Demosthenes' exile letters, for Demosthenes was subtly appealing for an amnesty in the hope of effecting his return (2, 10). He was unsuccessful.

The opening of the letter is unique in that it is in the form of a prayer, and the customary greeting to the Council and Assembly comes at the beginning of the second section, not at the start.[5] Goldstein (1968, pp. 176–178) explains this as the author needing to invoke the gods because of the significance of the circumstances that led to the letter (especially the call for what must have been an unpopular amnesty), and he draws attention to the introductory prayers in speeches (cf. Dem. 18.1 and 8).

Letter 1. On Political Harmony

[1] In starting anything of importance, either in speech or in action, I think it right to begin with the gods. Therefore, I pray to all the gods and goddesses that I may discern and write the best course of action for the people of Athens and those who are well disposed to the democracy, both now and in the future, and that the Athenians gathered in Assembly will adopt it. Having made this prayer, and with hopes of good inspiration from the gods, I send you this letter.

[2] Demosthenes sends greetings to the Council and Assembly. I think that you can deliberate at any time on the subject of my return home, and thus at this time I am not writing anything about it. However, I see that the present occasion can, if you choose the right course, bring glory and safety and freedom together, not only for you but also for all other Greeks, but that if you are guided by ignorance or led astray you will not easily find the same opportunity again; hence, I decided I should put my opinion about this matter before you.[6] [3] It is

---

[4] Demosthenes was not alone, for it appears that the general Leosthenes also made a speech to end dissension: see Grenfell and Hunt 1906, pp. 55–61, no. 15.

[5] "I send you this letter" at the end of 1 indicates that this is deliberate.

[6] Sections 2–4 are designed to capture the goodwill of the audience (*captatio benevolentiae*), the rhetorical function of the opening (*prooimion*) of a work; cf. M. de Brauw 2006.

hard to give effective advice by letter,[7] for you usually oppose many arguments rather than wait to understand them. A speaker can perceive what you want and easily correct your misapprehensions, but a written text has no such assistance against those who raise an uproar.[8] Nevertheless, if you are willing to listen to what I say in silence and have the patience to understand everything, I think that—may the gods support what I say—it will be clear that I am doing my duty on your behalf with all goodwill, and I will make clear what your interest is. [4] I decided to send this letter not because you were short on politicians or people who glibly and without calculation say whatever occurs to them. However, I wanted to make it clear to those who choose to speak what things I happen to know through experience and from following public affairs, and thus give them many starting points for considering what I take to be in your best interests, and to make the choice of the best procedures easier for the people. This then is why I was prompted to write the letter.

[5] Gentlemen of Athens, first of all you must agree among yourselves about the common interests of the city and put aside disputes with previous Assemblies. Second, you must all agree with the proposals you have endorsed and support them zealously, since not following one policy uniformly is not only unworthy of you and ignoble, but also holds the greatest dangers. [6] You must not neglect one thing which by itself is not enough to give you mastery of events but which, when added to your military strength, will make it easier to achieve everything else. What is this? That you not be bitter or bear a grudge towards any city or towards any citizen in one of those cities who has supported the current order.[9] [7] For the fear of this transforms those who know that they are part of that regime and face obvious danger into zealous supporters of the current order; but when

---

[7] On the difficulties of conveying advice by letter, cf. Isoc., *Letter* 1.2–3. There are also echoes of some of the arguments against writing in Alcidamas, *Against the Sophists*.

[8] On uproar (*thorubos*), see *Prologue* 26.1n.

[9] The "current order" here is a euphemism for the Macedonian hegemony of Greece established by Philip by means of the League of Corinth after Chaeronea (see the Introduction). Usually, the phrase means the constitution of an autonomous Greek *polis* (cf. Lys. 25.3).

they lose this fear they will all become more moderate—and this is no small benefit. Now, to proclaim such a policy in every city would be foolish, in fact impossible; but however you are seen treating your own citizens so you will also create in everyone's minds the expectation of similar treatment of others. [8] I say that you must not blame or condemn in any way whatsoever any general or orator[10] or private individual who before now seemed to support the current order, but concede to everyone in the city that they conducted public affairs as was necessary, seeing how the gods have done us a favor and saved our city, thereby giving you the opportunity to decide anew what you want to do. Imagine if you were on a ship and some were advocating using the sails and others the oars; although everything said by both parties is directed to the ship's safety, the opportunity to use either means depends on events controlled by the gods. [9] If you evaluate past events in this way, you will become trusted by all men, your actions will be those of good and honorable men, you will benefit your own affairs not a little, and either you will make all your opponents in the cities change their minds or only very few of them—the ringleaders—will be left. Therefore, carry out the common interest with vision and leadership, and do not think of your own private interests.

[10] I exhort you to act in this way, although I myself was not treated with such kindness by some people, but I was unjustly and for partisan reasons handed over for the pleasure of others.[11] However, I do not think that I should indulge my private resentment and so hurt the common good, nor should I mix my private enmity with the public interest, but what I am exhorting other men to do, I think I myself should be the first to do.

[11] The preparations and the precautions we need to take, and the course of action that, as far as human calculation can tell, is most likely to succeed, have been more or less said by me. However,

---

[10] The Athenians did not have a word for politician as we do; the most commonly used term was the phrase *rhētores kai stratēgoi* (orators and generals).

[11] The metaphor comes from the reckless giving of presents when drinking toasts at banquets. Demosthenes seems to have been a teetotaler, to judge from his comments about drinking water (6.30, 19.46; cf. Athenaeus 10.424d), and so his use of wine-drinking imagery here to express his disapproval of what happened to him is even more effective.

administering daily affairs, dealing properly with events that arise out of the blue, [**12**] knowing the right moment for everything, and judging which of our objectives can be attained through diplomacy and which need force in addition, these are the jobs of the generals who are in command. For this reason, giving advice places one in a very difficult position. For measures that are correctly planned and considered with much care and effort are often wrecked by the mismanagement of those appointed to oversee them. [**13**] For now, I hope that all will go well. If anyone thought that Alexander was fortunate because he succeeded in everything, let him consider that his good fortune came not from sitting still but from acting and working hard and daring. Now that he is dead, Fortune is seeking other people with whom to ally, and you should be these people.[12] [**14**] Appoint the most loyal leaders at the head of your forces, for they must manage your affairs.[13] And whatever each of you is able and willing to do, let him make a promise to himself and do it. See to it that he does not break that promise or fail to do his duty, claiming that he has been unduly deceived or misled, [**15**] because you will not find others to make up the deficiency where you yourselves fall short. Nor do frequent changes of mind bring the same danger in matters where it is in your power to act as you wish about matters that involve war, where a change of mind defeats your purpose. Do not do anything like this. However, whatever you resolve to do nobly and promptly with all your heart, vote for that, [**16**] and, once you have approved it, make your leaders Zeus of Dodona[14] and the other gods, who have given you many good, noble, and true oracles. Ask for their help, when you have prayed to all of them, pledging the prizes of victory, then with good luck set free the Greeks. Good luck.

---

[12] The Greeks were quick to identify Fortune (*tychē*) as responsible for successes and setbacks. Thus, the Athenians' defeat at Chaeronea was due to Fortune (Dem. 18.192–193; Hyp. 5.28–30; Plut., *Demosthenes* 21.1); cf. *Letter* 2.23, and esp. *Letter* 4.3 on Good Fortune living in Athens and how that will improve Athenian prospects. See also *Erotic Essay* 14, 32–33, 39; *Prologue* 2.

[13] Probably a reference to Phocion, who had been against the Greek revolt on Alexander's death; hence, his possible generalship would have been detrimental to the Athenians' war effort.

[14] On Demosthenes' exploitation of the oracle of Dodonian Zeus elsewhere, cf. 19.298–299 and Din. 1.78, 98–99. On the oracle, see *Letter* 4.3.

LETTER 2. CONCERNING HIS OWN RETURN

Introduction

For the background to Demosthenes' role in the Harpalus affair and his exile, see the Introduction. The content of this letter is clear from its title: Demosthenes protests that he was wrongly condemned when so many of those accused were acquitted on the same evidence (1–2, 15–16, 26), and he wants to return home. We do not have his defense speech from the trial, but if we compare the prosecution speeches of Dinarchus and Hyperides, it is plausible to assume that the letter repeats many of the arguments advanced in it. For example, Dinarchus' and Hyperides' speeches argue against Demosthenes' claim (cf. Letter 2.3–6, 10–12) that his political career was beneficial for Athens and for Greece (Din. 1.12–36, 70–71; Hyp. 5.16–26), and they often accuse him of taking bribes (Din. 1.18–28, 41–47, 70, 108; Hyp. 5.14, 17, 25), which he denies (7–8, 11, 14). Despite the straightforward style of this letter (in contrast to the third), it still contains much emotional rhetoric as Demosthenes tries to move the Athenians to pity by talking of his suffering and homesickness (1–2, 13–14, 17–25). This strategy may have had the opposite effect if Plutarch's critical reaction to it is anything to go by (*Demosthenes* 26.2 and 5). In any case, Demosthenes was not recalled.

At *Letter* 3.1 Demosthenes talks of a letter he has sent to Athens apparently protesting his innocence in the Harpalus affair, and at 3.37 he promises a "long letter" that the Athenians will receive describing his grievances. This longer one appears to be the second letter, and so it was written after the third (see further Goldstein 1968, pp. 48–58).

Letter 2. Concerning His Own Return

[1] Demosthenes to the Council and the Assembly sends greetings. In view of my previous conduct in political affairs, I used to think that, since I had done you no wrong, I would not suffer this sort of treatment, but that even if I had made a small mistake I would be pardoned.[15] But since it has turned out like this, as long as I observed

---

[15] Hyperides said in his prosecution speech that Demosthenes admitted he took money from Harpalus (5.12–13), and elsewhere he condemns Demosthenes

you condemning everyone on the basis of the secret report of the Council, without any clear proof or evidence from that body, I decided to make the best of it, thinking that you were surrendering your own privileges as much as depriving me of mine. For when the jurors bound by their oath[16] accept what the Council says without any evidence, they are abandoning the Constitution. [2] But since you have rightly discovered the power that some of those in the Council have secured for themselves,[17] and you are deciding cases according to the evidence, and have found that the secret activities of these men deserve condemnation, I think that, if you are willing, I should obtain the same release as those who faced the same charges, and should not be the only man to be deprived of his country, his property, and the company of his closest relatives because of a false accusation.[18]

[3] Gentlemen of Athens, you would be right to be concerned about my return not only because of the horrific treatment I received, despite having done you no wrong, but also for the sake of your reputation among other people. For you must not suppose that, just because no one reminds you of the times and circumstances in which I rendered the greatest services to the city, [4] the other Greeks are ignorant of these or have forgotten what I did on your behalf. I am reluctant right now to write in detail about my services for two reasons; first, because I am afraid of jealousy, against which it is pointless to speak the truth, and second, we are now forced to do many things unworthy of those services because of the cowardice of the other Greeks. [5] In brief, the services I did on your behalf and for which I was examined were such that you were envied by all, and I hoped to receive the greatest rewards from you. And when fate, irresistible and unfeeling, decided the war for the freedom of

---

for corruption (5.11, 15, 24–26; cf. 34–36), as does Dinarchus (1.22–26, 60, 68–71, 88, 93).

[16] Every year, each juror swore an oath to uphold the laws (Dem. 24.149–151): see MacDowell 1978, pp. 44 and 60.

[17] According to Dinarchus (1.62) and Hyperides (5.14), Demosthenes had said he was the victim of a plot by some members of the Areopagus.

[18] Apart from Demosthenes, only Demades and Philocles were found guilty. When Demosthenes was fined, his property was confiscated by the state. For a similar appeal, cf. *Letter* 3.40.

Greece,[19] in which you yourselves contended, not as justice required but as it wished, [6] in the aftermath of this I did not renounce my goodwill towards you, nor exchange it for anything else, not for favor, or hope, or wealth, or power, or security,[20] although I saw that those who were willing to take part in public life against your interests were receiving all of these.

[7] Among the many important reasons why I am confident I can speak freely, I think the most important is this, and I will not hesitate to write it to you. Of all those remembered throughout time, Philip was the most skilled at using his personal powers to persuade men to pay attention to his wishes[21] and at using bribes to corrupt the leading politicians in each of the Greek cities.[22] [8] But I alone did not succumb to either method, and this is a matter of pride for you.[23] Although I met Philip many times and discussed with him matters on which you sent me as your envoy, I refrained from taking the huge sums he offered me, as many men still alive know.[24] Consider what opinion these men probably have of you. The treatment you have inflicted on a man like me, I know well, seems for me a misfortune, not

---

[19] A reference to the Battle of Chaeronea in 338: see the Introduction. That it was Fortune that caused Athens' defeat is found in other sources; cf. Hyp. 5.28–30; Plut., *Demosthenes* 21; Polybius 29.21.

[20] Demosthenes left Athens after Chaeronea on the pretext of securing grain, and he was criticized for this at his trial in 323 (cf. Din. 1.80–82).

[21] A possible reference to Aeschines' having been won over by Philip. Although Aeschines left Athens in 330, Demosthenes might not have been able to resist a dig at him.

[22] Philip was not averse to bribing officials to achieve his objectives, and Demosthenes says that he had tried to bribe him when he was at the Macedonian court in 346 (19.167). See also Din. 1.26 and Diodorus Siculus 16.53.2; cf. Dem. 1.5, 8.40, 9.56–57, 19.265, 342, 18.48.

[23] Demosthenes was often accused of accepting bribes (cf. Aes. 3.85, 103, 156, 173, 209, 238–240, 259; Din. 1.10, 15, 28, 41–45, 70; Hyp. 5.25). These may have been gifts and not actual bribes, for receiving gifts was part of Greek diplomacy: see Adcock and Mosley 1974, pp. 164–165, and Harvey 1985.

[24] Reference to Demosthenes' embassies to Philip in 346 in connection with the Peace of Philocrates. He later accused the king of bribing the other Athenian ambassadors (Dem. 19.167–168).

a sign of my corruption, but for you it is folly. Change your judgment and remove this impression.

[9] I consider everything that I have just said of less importance than the entire course of my political life each and every day, in which I showed myself to be a public servant who never gave way to anger or ill will or unjust gain, either public or private, never brought malicious accusations against a citizen or an alien, and never cleverly worked against you in private, but when the need arose I worked on your behalf and won public approval. [10] The older men would know—and it's only right that you tell the younger ones—about the Assembly meeting for Python of Byzantium,[25] when he came with the envoys from the Greeks, to show that the city was acting wrongly, but left when he achieved the opposite effect, after I alone of the speakers at that time defended your rights in the matter. I omit all the embassies on which I served on your behalf, in which you never suffered any disadvantage, not even one.[26] [11] For the aim of my policy, gentlemen of Athens, was not to see how you could defeat one another, or to incite the city against itself, but for you to acquire a reputation for honesty and generosity. All of you, especially the young, should admire these things, and look not only for the man who in every way strives to win your favor (for there is never a shortage of this type of person), but also for the man who will loyally criticize you for your ignorance.

[12] I pass over many things for which another man, even without any other useful services, would rightly expect to be restored—providing a chorus and a trireme and giving out money on all occasions.[27]

---

[25] Python came to Athens in 344 accompanied by representatives of Philip's allies, carrying with him the king's intentions to alter the Peace of Philocrates by suggesting amendments "on the understanding that Philip would do whatever they voted for" ([Dem.] 7.21–22; cf. 18–23 and Dem. 18.136). Demosthenes successfully opposed Python in his second *Philippic* oration (6).

[26] On Demosthenes' embassies, see Dem. 18.219–222 (to which add his one to Nicanor at Olympia over the Exiles Decree: see the Introduction).

[27] Public services or liturgies (such as maintaining a ship for one year or providing a chorus for a dramatic performance) were paid for by wealthy Athenians out of their own funds and were often used as a stepping stone into political life. Demosthenes' liturgies and other public gifts over his career were enormous: see the Series Introduction. For a different view, see Din. 1.96.

As far as these services go, you will find not only did I do my part first but also I exhorted others to do likewise. Gentlemen of Athens, consider each of my services and see how undeserved is the misfortune I now suffer.

[13] My current troubles are so plentiful that I am at a loss which one to deplore first. Will it be my old age[28] in which I am forced to experience the dangers of exile for the first time in my life when I did not deserve it? Or, the shame of being convicted and ruined without any investigation or proof of guilt?[29] Or, the hopes that I have now lost and the evils I suffer that ought rightly to belong to others? [14] My previous political activity gave no just grounds for punishment, nor were the allegations at my trial proved. For it will be clear that I was never a friend of Harpalus, and of the decrees proposed concerning Harpalus, only mine made the city blameless.[30] It is evident from all of this that I was seized because of circumstances, not for any crime, and that by coming into court first, I unjustly incurred the anger directed against all those included in the charges.[31] [15] For which of the pleas that saved those who were later tried did I not myself state? What proof of guilt did the Council[32] cite against me? Or what could it now cite? There is none; for it is impossible to make facts out of what never happened. However, I will stop going on about these, although I could write much. For I have learned by experience that the consciousness of innocence is of little help, but is the most painful way of all to increase my suffering. [16] Since you have become

---

[28] Demosthenes was born in 384/3, and so he was now about 60.

[29] A reference to Demosthenes' condemnation in the Harpalus affair by the Areopagus despite the lack of evidence against him: see the Introduction.

[30] Demosthenes proposed to imprison Harpalus, to confiscate his money and establish a guard over it, perhaps to send an embassy to Alexander, and to inquire into the missing money after Harpalus escaped; cf. Din. 1.62 and 82.

[31] Demosthenes was the first of at least six men to be tried: Din. 1.105–106 (cf. 113); Hyp. 5.6–7. For the disadvantages of being tried first, cf. Lys. 19.6: "You can see this most clearly when many people face trial on the same charge, because what generally happens is that those who are tried last are acquitted" (Todd's translation in *Lysias* in this series).

[32] This was the Areopagus.

properly reconciled with all those indicted in the charges,[33] be reconciled with me as well, gentlemen of Athens. I have never done you any wrong, as the gods and heroes testify.[34] And all time down to this very moment is my witness, which you should more rightly believe than the unsupported charge recently brought against me. You will find that I am neither the worst nor the least trustworthy of those falsely accused.

[17] Surely my flight[35] should not cause you to grow angry with me, for I left not because I renounced you or was looking to switch my allegiance elsewhere,[36] but because first it was hard to bear the disgrace of imprisonment, and second, because of my old age, my body was not able to endure the hardships. Moreover, I did not think that you were unwilling for me to escape from the mudslinging, which brought you no benefit and was destroying me. [18] You could see many signs that I was loyal to you and to no one else. I did not go to a city in which I was likely to perform outstanding services but to one where I knew our ancestors had gone when faced by the danger from Persia[37] and which I was aware had a friendly disposition towards you. [19] That city is Troezen,[38] and may all the gods be especially kind to it because of its goodwill to you and its kindness to me; and may I be able to return the

---

[33] Of the others who were convicted, we know that Demades was back in Athens by the time of Alexander's death (Plut., *Phocion* 22.3). We know nothing about the fate of Philocles or those others who may have been convicted.

[34] Such invocations to the demigods or semidivine ancestors of noble families and to the gods generally are common in oratory; cf. Lyc. 1.1.

[35] Demosthenes fled into exile after one week in prison. *Letter* 3.40–42 and [Plut.], *Moralia* 846c, say that he left because he was unable to pay his fine.

[36] That is, Macedonia.

[37] Shortly before the Battle of Salamis in 480, the Athenian men collected together with the fleet at Salamis while the women and children were sent to Troezen (Herod. 8.41.1; Hyp. 3.31–32; Plut., *Themistocles* 10.3), which is in the Peloponnese, directly across the Saronic Gulf from Athens.

[38] After the Battle of Chaeronea in 338 the Athenians sought an alliance with Troezen, but Philip established a pro-Macedonian oligarchy there (Aelian, *Varia Historia* 6.1). The Athenians took in the expelled citizens (Hyp. 3.31). The oligarchy in Troezen must have been overthrown by the time of this letter, for if Demosthenes had gone there, he would have mentioned it.

favor when I am acquitted by you. When some men in this city, in an effort to gratify me, condemned you for acting against me in ignorance, I exercised complete discretion, as was proper. And I think that this was mainly why they all admired me and honored me publicly.

[20] Seeing that the goodwill of these men was great, but that they had little power to affect their present circumstances, I went to the sanctuary of Poseidon at Calauria[39] where I settled not only for my safety, which I hope is assured me because of the god (I am not certain about that; for the safety of a man in jeopardy is weak and unclear when it is in the hands of others who may do as they wish), but also because from here each day I can gaze at my country, towards which I know I have as much affection as I pray I may have from you.

[21] Therefore, gentlemen of Athens, so that I am no longer afflicted by these present miseries, vote to give me what you have given for certain others, so that I do not suffer anything unworthy of you or be forced to become a suppliant of others, for that would not be good for you. Indeed, if the differences between you and me remain irreconcilable, then it would be better for me to be dead. [22] You should believe that I am in this frame of mind and am not now boasting idly. For I put myself in your hands, and I did not flee from the trial, for I did not want to betray the truth or deprive any of you of your authority over me, but I wanted you to do as you wished with me. For I thought that those from whom I received all my fame and fortune should also have the right to do me wrong, if they wished. [23] Since in doing good a just fortune prevailed over the unjust and has given you the chance to deliberate the same issues twice, for nothing in the verdict is unalterable, save me, gentlemen of Athens, and cast votes that are worthy of yourselves and of me. [24] You will find that I have done no wrong in any of my actions, nor do I deserve to be disfranchised or ruined.[40] Indeed, I have as much goodwill to the people as anyone has (not to write anything invidious); of those alive now, I have achieved the most on your behalf, and of my contemporaries I show the strongest signs of loyalty to you.

---

[39] This temple was supposed to offer inviolable sanctuary for those in need; Calauria is modern Poros. At the end of the Lamian War Demosthenes again fled to this sanctuary, and it was there that he committed suicide (Plut., *Demosthenes* 29.1).

[40] As a convicted criminal, Demosthenes lost his voting and legal rights.

[25] Gentlemen of Athens, let not one of you imagine that I express my grief throughout the whole of this letter from cowardice or from any other base reason. Each man is endlessly occupied with his present circumstances, but what faces me now (if only this had never happened!) are grief and tears, a yearning for my country and for you, and the thought of what I have suffered, all of which make me grieve.[41] Consider everything fairly; you will find neither weakness nor cowardice in any of my political activities on your behalf.

[26] So much is directed to all of you; but I want to say something to those who malign me in front of you.[42] What they did in submitting to your ignorant actions, I will concede they did because of you, and I do not complain. But since you now recognize these things for what they are, if they make the same concession to me as they allow in the case of the others, they will act well. However, if they attempt to be malicious, I ask all of you to help me, and not to let their enmity prevail over your gratitude to me. Good luck.

LETTER 3. CONCERNING THE SONS OF LYCURGUS

Introduction

Despite Lycurgus' reputation and great services to Athens, especially in the financial sphere,[43] he was indicted towards the end of his life by

---

[41] The invocation of pity here echoes the call for pity at the start of the letter; cf. the epilogue of *Letter* 3.

[42] Probably Hyperides and his faction, who had a more overtly militant policy to Macedonia than Demosthenes, and, after the latter's political disgrace in the Harpalus affair, were now politically powerful. Hyperides had also prosecuted Demosthenes in 323 and had been responsible for persuading the Athenians to revolt after Alexander's death. Demosthenes ends his letter by appealing to the people *en masse* in an effort to offset Hyperides' influence and so effect his recall; cf. *Letter* 3.29–30, 34.

[43] On Lycurgus, see the Introduction, the Introduction to Lycurgus in *Dinarchus, Hyperides, and Lycurgus* in this series; Mitchel 1970; and Bosworth 1988, pp. 204–214. There is a brief life of him at [Plut.], *Moralia* 841a–844a, and his accomplishments are listed in the honorary decree proposed by Stratocles (*IG* ii² 457 = [Plut.], *Moralia* 851f–852e). He became treasurer of the Theoric Fund in probably 336 and remained in charge of Athens' finances until 324. In 330 he prosecuted Leocrates for deserting Athens after Chaeronea, but he was unsuccessful.

the Macedonian sympathizer Menesaechmus, who succeeded him as Athens' chief financial officer. The charge was unknown, but it may have been embezzlement of some type, given his previous control of Athens' finances. Since Lycurgus' incorruptibility and adherence to the laws were legendary,[44] the charge was probably a sham. Menesaechmus seems to have been an opponent of the anti-Macedonians in this period, and he was also one of Demosthenes' prosecutors at his trial in 323. It is possible that he prosecuted Lycurgus because of his association with Demosthenes. Personal reasons may also have played a role, for some time earlier Lycurgus had successfully prosecuted Menesaechmus on a religious charge. At his trial, Lycurgus was carried into court on his deathbed, but he successfully defended himself. Not long after, he died. Menesaechmus then had Thrasycles indict Lycurgus' sons for their father's alleged crime[45] and prosecuted them himself. They were convicted and imprisoned.

This letter is a brilliant piece of work by Demosthenes. It was written to plead the release of Lycurgus' sons, yet only about three-quarters of it dealt with that issue. Instead, Demosthenes exploited the opportunity to plead his recall, and he cleverly wove into the letter's content seemingly general allusions to himself (what we may call "subliminal suggestions"); for example, 9–10, 15, 18, 27.

The letter is in the form of a *dēmegoria* that in Anaximenes is classed as "coming to the aid of the distressed, whether private individuals or city states" (*Rhetorica ad Alexandrum* 34). Demosthenes begins by gaining the goodwill of the audience (*captatio benevolentiae*), followed by a brief narrative of Lycurgus' career (2–10), which extends the *pro-oimion,* just as Anaximenes recommends when someone was faced

---

His prosecution speech has survived; see *Dinarchus, Hyperides, and Lycurgus* (cited above).

[44] [Plut.], *Moralia* 842b, tells us that Lycurgus' wife disobeyed the law that no woman should go to Eleusis in a carriage and that Lycurgus rewarded those who informed on her with a talent. Cf. [Plut.], *Moralia* 841f: "Throughout his life he was always highly esteemed among the Athenians and considered a just man, so that in the lawcourts the word of Lycurgus was seen as a help to anyone who needed an advocate."

[45] Under Athenian law, Menesaechmus was prevented from indicting them himself because Lycurgus had been acquitted.

by difficult circumstances (*Rhetorica ad Alexandrum* 31). Demosthenes bases his arguments on justice (2–4) and expediency (5–10), and he echoes criticisms of the Athenians by other Greeks by the use of the rhetorical device of *fictio personarum* ("making another speak in our place").[46] In doing so, he widens the context to one affecting the Athenians' reputation in Greece as a whole.

Sections 11–34 are the proof (*confirmatio*), in which Demosthenes criticizes the Athenians for their treatment of a democrat like Lycurgus. He is less interested in Lycurgus as an administrator and more in his reputation, and hence how the Athenians show the wrong attitude towards democrats by making him and his sons suffer unjustly.

Rather than close the letter with a final appeal for the children, as might be expected, Demosthenes uses the epilogue (35–45) to describe aspects of his own treatment. He also urges his own return by exploiting the emotions, especially pity[47] (including a masterful comparison of himself with the disreputable Aristogeiton at 37 and 42–43). By appealing on behalf of Lycurgus' sons, Demosthenes rebukes the Athenians and stresses that he cares as much about the city's reputation as about his own exoneration. That allows him to talk about his own treatment and hence to plead for his recall.

Although there was some attempt in Athens to free Lycurgus' children,[48] Demosthenes' letter was instrumental in securing their release. However, he was not successful in effecting his own return with this letter; that would not happen for several more months, probably in the winter of 323/2.

This was probably the second letter that Demosthenes wrote when in exile. He refers at the start to one he had sent Athens in connection with the Harpalus affair, and at 37 he promises to send a "long letter" with further details of his innocence in that affair. Since the longer letter appears to be Letter 2, we may place the third, on behalf of Lycurgus' sons, chronologically before the second one (see further Goldstein 1968, pp. 48–58).

---

[46] See Arist., *Rhetoric* 3.17; cf. Quintilian 9.2.29–30.

[47] Cf. also the epilogue of *Letter 2*.

[48] We have a fragment of a speech by Hyperides: *Dinarchus, Hyperides, and Lycurgus* in this series, Fr. 31, p. 145.

Letter 3. Concerning the Sons of Lycurgus

[1] Demosthenes to the Council and the Assembly sends greetings. I sent you an earlier letter about my own affairs,[49] and what I considered the right thing to do—which you will agree to do only when you think fit. I should not want you to ignore what I now write nor to receive it in a partisan way but to give it a just hearing. For, while spending time away from you, I happened to hear many people criticizing you for how you are treating the sons of Lycurgus. [2] In fact, I would have sent you this letter anyway because of what he did when he was alive, for which you would all rightly be grateful to him as I am if you chose to act properly. At the start of his career he devoted himself to the financial administration of the state[50] and did not develop the practice of proposing measures concerning the Greeks and their allies.[51] However, when most of those pretending to be friends of democracy were deserting you, he attached himself to the people's interests [3] not because he might receive gifts and rewards from them, for all such benefits were coming from the opposite side, nor because he observed that this choice was safer—for a man electing to speak on the people's behalf necessarily faced many clear dangers—, but because he was a democrat and by nature a man of honor. [4] And yet he observed firsthand that those who would have helped the people were weakened by events, while those on the other side became stronger in every respect. Nevertheless, he held firm to policies that he thought were in the best interests of the people, and from then on he was conspicuous in saying and doing

---

[49] This letter does not survive.

[50] Lycurgus held the crucially important office of Treasurer of the Theoric Fund, into which all budget surpluses were paid. In the fourth century it was a substantial financial reserve, so that the officials who controlled it wielded great political power. There was even a law that inflicted death on anyone who proposed that it be used for military purposes in peacetime: see Dem. 10.35–45; cf. 14.24–28. See further Buchanan 1962.

[51] Lycurgus was not very good at public speaking, and he used an Olynthian man named Eucleides to propose measures in the Assembly ([Plut.], *Moralia* 842c). However, we know of one decree proposed by Lycurgus himself to honor Eudemus of Plataea in 330/29 (*IG* ii² 351).

the right thing. For this, his surrender was immediately demanded, as everyone knows.[52]

[5] As I said at the outset, I would have written this letter simply in gratitude to Lycurgus himself; but because I also thought it would help you to know the recriminations coming from foreigners, I became even more eager to send this letter. I beseech those who in private are hostile to him to listen patiently to a true and just account of him. Gentlemen of Athens, know well that the city is getting a bad reputation now from your treatment of this man's children. [6] For every Greek knows that while Lycurgus was alive, you gave him extraordinary honors, and although he was indicted many times by those who envied him, you never found a single allegation true, and had such confidence in him and considered him more devoted to the people than anyone else that you decided many issues of justice by Lycurgus' word alone, and this was enough for you. This would not have happened if you had not held the same view as he. [7] Therefore, all men who now hear that his sons are in chains[53] pity the dead father, sympathize with the children whose treatment is undeserved, and reproach you with bitter words that I would not dare to write down. I am angry at what they say, and in your defense I refute them as best as I am able; I have written down only as much as will show you that many blame you, for I think it better for you to know this, but I judge that reporting their exact words would be disagreeable. [8] Apart from the abuse, however, I will reveal what some people say and what I think would be advantageous for you to hear. No one imagines that you act from ignorance or are deceived about the truth about Lycurgus himself. For the long period of time during which he was investigated,[54] and never found to have wronged you in

---

[52] After Thebes revolted from Macedonia and was destroyed in 335, Alexander demanded the surrender of several of the leading Athenian statesmen, including Demosthenes and Lycurgus, who had supported the revolt: see the Introduction. Demosthenes refers to it here to show not only that Lycurgus was a good democrat but also to remind his audience that he too was a democrat when Alexander had demanded him.

[53] The verb in Greek here (*dedesthai*) could also mean "in prison," as Demosthenes wants to evoke a pitiful picture of Lycurgus' sons; cf. 12 and 13 below.

[54] This probably refers to the investigation that a public official underwent when his term of office expired. If found derelict in his duty, he would be indicted (cf. Dem. 18.246).

thought or action, and the fact that no man has accused you of apathy in any other matter naturally rules out the excuse of ignorance.

[9] Therefore, all that is left is what everyone would call the behavior of despicable men—you seem to care for a man so long as you can use him, and after that, you no longer give him any thought. For in what other way should one expect you to show favor to a dead man when that person sees the opposite conduct towards his children and his reputation, which are the only things where well-being is a concern to all men after death? [10] And indeed to do these things for the sake of money is also not the mark of good and honorable men, for this would clearly not be consistent with either your magnanimity or your principles. For if you had to ransom the children from other people and to give this amount of money from your revenues,[55] I think you all would be eager to do it. However, when I see that you are averse to canceling a fine imposed from rumor and envy, I do not know what opinion I can hold, except that you have embarked on a bitter and confused course against democrats. If this is so, then you have decided to deliberate wrongly and against your best interests.

[11] I am astonished that none of you thinks that it would be disgraceful if the people of Athens, who are thought to exceed everyone in natural intelligence and education (*paideia*),[56] and who have always offered a common refuge to those in trouble,[57] appear to be less compassionate than Philip, who, though probably badly instructed and brought up without any restriction, [12] nevertheless thought he should display a most generous spirit at the time of his greatest success[58] and did not dare to chain his opponents in battle, against whom he had risked everything, after learning who they and their fathers were. For unlike some of your orators, it seems, he thought it would be neither

---

[55] We are not told how much the fine was, but it was a large one. The children were imprisoned until it was paid.

[56] The remark recalls that of Pericles in his funeral oration, that Athens was the "school (*paideusis*) of Hellas" (Thuc. 2.41.1).

[57] Athens as a place of refuge is a common theme in oratory (cf. Aes. 3.134; Dem. 57.6; Isoc. 4.52, 8.138).

[58] This was the Battle of Chaeronea in 338. After his victory, Philip treated the Athenians, who expected him to march on the city, with leniency; see the Introduction and cf. the Introduction to *Funeral Oration.*

just nor honorable to treat everyone the same, but he took into account the additional factor of their worth when judging such matters. [**13**] Although as Athenians and living in a culture which, it is believed, can make even dull people bearable, you first—and this is the most cruel of all your actions—put the sons in chains because of crimes that some people allege against their father;[59] second, you say that this is equal treatment, as if you were determining the equality of weights and measures, not deliberating about the moral and political conduct of men. [**14**] In examining this sort of conduct, if the deeds of Lycurgus appear to have been democratic and motivated by goodwill, then it is only right that you should do his sons no harm but grant them every good thing. However, if his deeds are the opposite, then he should have been punished while he was alive, but even so his children should not incur your anger for crimes that someone alleges against their father; for death is the end of all crimes to all men. [**15**] You feel that those who dislike statesmen who support democracy should not be reconciled with them even when they are dead but should also maintain their hatred for their children, then the people, in whose cause every good democrat joins, will remember their indebtedness only while they can use his help, and after that will not care at all. In that case, nothing will be more miserable than to choose the side of the people.

[**16**] If Moerocles[60] answers that this line is too subtle for him, and that he himself put them in chains so that they would not escape, ask him about the time when Taureas,[61] Pataecus,[62] Aristogeiton,[63] and he

---

[59] What Lycurgus was charged with is unknown, but he was acquitted; see the Introduction to this letter.

[60] Moerocles, archon in 324 and one of the statesmen demanded by Alexander in 335 (see 3.4n), was one of the Eleven (a type of police force) who imprisoned Lycurgus' sons. If Demosthenes is right in 16–17 that Moerocles was himself a criminal, then he was holding his office and speaking to the Assembly illegally. On the Eleven, see Burgess 2005.

[61] Nothing is known about Taureas, except that he seems to have been a glutton (Athenaeus 8.342f, 8.343d, 10.416f).

[62] Pataecus was from Eleusis and in addition to some public duties may have been a priest of Asclepius in 345/4.

[63] Aristogeiton had a long criminal history. Lycurgus and Demosthenes indicted him for illegally prosecuting Ariston of Alopece, probably in 325/4, despite

himself were condemned to prison, and were not only not put in chains but also spoke in public; why did he not see the arguments for justice in that case? [**17**] If he says that he was not in office then, according to the laws he should not have made a speech. Consequently, how can it be equal treatment when some hold office when they are not permitted to speak, but others are in chains when their father served you well so many times? [**18**] I cannot understand this, unless you wish to make it clear in public that power in the city lies in brutality, shamelessness, and deliberate wrongdoing, and that these offer more hope for security, and that if these kinds of men get into trouble there is a way to escape, but that to elect to live a life of moderation and as a good democrat according to good principles is dangerous, and, if any mistake is made, there will be no escape.

[**19**] I will pass over the fact that it is wrong to have a contrary opinion of Lycurgus than you held while he was alive, but it is right to have more regard for the dead than the living and all other such considerations; for I take it that these are agreed upon by everyone. Nevertheless, I would be glad to see you bear in mind all the descendants of others whose ancestral deeds you remembered, such as the descendants of Aristeides,[64] Thrasybulus,[65] Archinus,[66] and many others. I have not brought these examples forward to criticize you—[**20**] far from it—

---

being *atimos* (deprived of his civic rights). The prosecution speeches attributed to Demosthenes exist (25 and 26), as do fragments of that by Lycurgus (*Dinarchus, Lycurgus, and Hyperides,* Fr. 2). Aristogeiton was also indicted in the Harpalus affair; Dinarchus 2 is the speech delivered against him, and it was successful. See also 37 and 42–43.

[64] Aristeides was a general during the Persian Wars (490–479), and in 478 he founded the Delian League, which led to the fifth-century Athenian empire (cf. Thuc. 1.96–97). He was later ostracized and apparently was so poor when he died that his funeral expenses were met by the state, which also provided for his children.

[65] When Athens was controlled by the Thirty in 404/3, Thrasybulus led the democratic opposition that defeated the Thirty at the Battle of Munychia in 403.

[66] Archinus was a supporter of Thrasybulus, but he blocked the former's promise of rewarding foreigners who supported the democratic opposition with Athenian citizenship. Demosthenes tells us (19.280–281 and 24.134, 135) that the descendants of Thrasybulus and Archinus were later fined and imprisoned for debt, but this is not necessarily inconsistent with their being rewarded in their youth.

but because I think that this practice is in the best interests of the city; for it allows you to challenge all men to be good democrats, since they see that even if envy prevents them from receiving their due honor in their own lifetime, their children, at any rate, will receive appropriate rewards from you.

[21] Is it not absurd, or indeed shocking, if certain other citizens who were considered useful a long time ago, whose good deeds you know from hearing about them, although you have not seen them yourselves, justly retain your goodwill, but to Lycurgus, whose political career and death are so recent, [22] you have not shown even the same degree of mercy or kindness as you eagerly did at other times to those who were obscure and who did you wrong? Not only that, but punishment has fallen on his children, whom even an enemy, if he were considerate and reasonable, would pity.

[23] I am also astonished that any of you does not know that it would not be in the best interests of our political affairs if it becomes known that those who have acquired the friendship of others[67] are not only likely to prosper in every way when they are successful, but also have an easier means of escape if misfortune strikes them, whereas those who side with the people not only are worse off but for them alone misfortune also remains inescapable. That this is the case is easy to show. [24] Which of you does not know what happened to Laches the son of Melanopus,[68] who was convicted in court in the same way as the sons of Lycurgus now, but the entire fine was revoked after Alexander's letter? And again, Mnesibulus of Acharnae[69] was condemned in the same way, when the court convicted him just as it had the children of Lycurgus, but he was let off, and rightly so, for he deserved to be? [25] In those cases none of those who now protest said that the laws were being subverted. Quite right too. The laws were not being subverted, if indeed all laws are enacted for the sake of justice and the security of good people, and it is advantageous that the troubles of the unfortunate should not be everlasting, and that you not be seen to appear ungrateful. [26] Moreover, if these principles are in

---

[67] That is, Macedonians.

[68] Laches belonged to a wealthy and prominent family, presumably with Macedonian sympathies.

[69] Nothing is known about Mnesibulus.

your best interests, as we would acknowledge, then not only did you not subvert the laws when you released those men but also you preserved the aims of the men who enacted the laws when you released Laches as a favor to Alexander, when he asked you to, and when you pardoned Mnesibulus because of his life of moderation.

[**27**] Do not show that it is more profitable for a person to acquire a foreign friend[70] than to entrust himself to the people, or that it is better to be an obscure person than to be known as a public figure working for the best interests of all of you. Someone who advises and otherwise works for the common good cannot please everyone; but if someone, out of loyalty, shares the interests of the people, it is right for him to be safe. Otherwise, you will teach everyone to serve others rather than the people, and to avoid becoming known as one who acts in your best interests. [**28**] Gentlemen of Athens, in a nutshell you all share the blame and the whole city experiences the misfortune if envy is considered more influential among you than gratitude for good service, especially when envy is a disease but gratitude has a place among the gods.

[**29**] Moreover, I will not leave out Pytheas,[71] who was a democrat until his recent switch,[72] after which he was willing to do everything against you. For who does not know that, when he began his political career on your side, he was persecuted as a slave and was indicted as an alien for assuming citizenship and was almost sold[73] by the same men in whose service he has written speeches against me? [**30**] However, he himself now does what he once prosecuted others for doing, and he is rich enough to have two mistresses, who serve him well by escorting him to his grave by consumption,[74] and he has paid off a debt of five

---

[70] That is, a Macedonian.

[71] Pytheas sided with Demosthenes in opposing Alexander's request for Athenian ships in 335 and his deification in 324. However, in 323 he was one of Demosthenes' prosecutors in the Harpalus affair, and after Alexander's death he switched allegiance and joined Antipater.

[72] The translation follows Goldstein's explanation of the Greek word *parodos* in the text (1968, pp. 224–225).

[73] If found guilty of illegally exercising one's political rights, a defendant lost his property and was sold as a slave.

[74] It is possible that the reference to the disreputable Pytheas and his mistresses is meant to evoke Hyperides, for at one time the latter had three mistresses,

talents more easily than he could produce five drachmas before. In addition, not only does he have from you, the people, the right to take part in public life, which is a disgrace common to all, but he also performs the ancestral sacrifices at Delphi on your behalf.[75]

[**31**] When everyone can see so many examples of this nature, and can judge from them that it does not pay to champion the cause of the people, I am afraid that you will have no one to speak for you, especially when mankind's natural fate, or fortune, or lapse of time has taken away some of the democrats, such as Nausicles,[76] Chares,[77] Diotimus,[78] Menestheus,[79] and Eudoxus,[80] as well as Euthydicus,[81]

---

including Myrrhina, the most expensive in the city ([Plut.], *Moralia* 849d; cf. Athenaeus 8.341e).

[75] Pytheas must have served (probably in spring 323) as an Athenian delegate to the Pythais at Delphi, and there taken part in an Amphictyonic sacrifice (the Amphictyony was the council of Greek states that managed the oracular site of Apollo at Delphi).

[76] Nausicles successfully defended Greece against the advance of Philip II at Thermopylae in 352 and served on the first embassy to Philip II in 346. In 326/5 he was a trierarch and his son, a syntrierarch (*IG* ii² 1628, 100–102; cf. Dem. 18.114).

[77] Chares fought on behalf of Athens in the Social War of 356–355 (see *Prologue* 2.3n16), sailed to help the people of Olynthus in 348 against Philip II, and then defended Greece (at Amphissa) against the Macedonian advance in 339/8. In the 320s he was in charge of a group of mercenaries at Taenarum, in southern Laconia, by then the main mercenary base in Greece. See also *Prologue* 37 and cf. *Prologue* 50n86 on the Social War.

[78] Diotimus came from a wealthy family. In addition to various liturgies (mostly as trierarch), he had a distinguished political and military career, serving as general at least twice (338/7 and 335/4) and honored by the Athenians for his campaign against pirates in 335/4. He was also one of the Athenians whom Alexander demanded in 335 (see *Letter* 3.4n).

[79] Menestheus was one of the Athenian commanders fighting rebellious allies in the Social War (see *Prologue* 2.3). He was general twice (356/5 and 333/2) and died by 325/4, for *IG* ii² 1629, 486–488 talks of his heirs paying off his naval debt.

[80] We know little about Eudoxus, other than he was a member of the Boule.

[81] Euthydicus is named only here and at Din. 1.33, which says that he was a democrat and that his association with Demosthenes led to his demise. Since his name occurs with that of Ephialtes in the only two ancient sources we have for him, he may have served on an embassy to Persia with Ephialtes (see next note).

Ephialtes,[82] and Lycurgus, and you yourselves have exiled others, such as Charidemus,[83] Philocles,[84] and myself. [32] Even you yourselves do not consider anyone else more loyal than these. I do not mind if you think that others are equally loyal, but I would like you to have as many as possible if you will deal fairly with them and not let them suffer the same fate as us. However, when you produce examples like these we now see, who will want to give himself genuinely to this democratic service? [33] You will have no shortage of men who pretend to be like this, just as there has been none in the past. God forbid I would live to see them unmasked like those men, who now openly follow policies that they once repudiated, feeling neither fear nor shame in front of you. Gentlemen of Athens, you must consider all this. Do not take lightly those who are loyal, and do not listen to those who are leading the state into bitterness and cruelty. [34] For our present affairs need goodwill and consideration for others far more than dissension and malice. Some men exploit these faults to make a profit against your interests in anticipation of the future; I hope their calculations will turn out false. If one of you disparages these warnings, then he is wholly naïve.[85] For if that person sees things happening that no one would have expected, would

---

[82] Ephialtes served on an embassy to Persia in 341/0 and returned with monetary support for a war against Philip II. He was one of those statesmen demanded by Alexander in 335, but he left Athens, for he was later found serving under Memnon of Rhodes and was killed while helping to defend Halicarnassus in 334.

[83] Charidemus was from Oreus on Euboea, but he was granted Athenian citizenship for his military services. Much information on Charidemus' life is found in Dem. 23.144–195. Aeschines says that he was the first man to send news of Philip II's death to Athens (3.77), and he was one of those demanded by Alexander in 335 (see *Letter* 3.4n52). Although the king relented in this demand for the others, he insisted on Charidemus' surrender. Charidemus went to Persia, where he was executed in 333.

[84] Philocles held a number of important military commands and was the general of Munychia and the dockyards who admitted Harpalus into Athens in 324, for which he was brought to trial: see the Introduction. Dinarchus' speech (3) from his trial survives: see *Dinarchus, Hyperides, and Lycurgus*.

[85] Demosthenes in this section may well mean Hyperides, who was famous for his skill at ridicule (*diasurmos*): see [Longinus], *On the Sublime* 34.2 and Whitehead 2000, pp. 10–18.

he not be mad if he thinks that what happened before, when the people were set against those speaking on their behalf by men enlisted for this purpose, could not happen now?

[35] If I were present, I would explain these things to you with my own voice, but since I am in a position in which I wish anyone who slandered me to the point of ruin might find himself, I have written what I want to say in a letter; first, in consideration of your honor and well-being, and second, because I consider it right to show that I have the same goodwill towards Lycurgus' sons as I had towards him when he was alive. [36] If it has occurred to anyone that I have many troubles of my own, I would not hesitate to say to him that I am as concerned about my own safety as I am about your best interests and not deserting any of my friends. Thus, I do not write because of my abundance of troubles, but I attend to both your affairs and my own with a single purpose and from conviction. And the many troubles I have are of the kind I would wish on those who are plotting evil against you. However, I have said enough about this.

[37] I would like to explain my complaint against you in a spirit of goodwill and friendship, briefly for the moment, but a little later in a long letter,[86] which you may expect, if I live long enough, unless you treat me with justice before then. You are—what can I say that would not be a lie or misleading?—you are thoughtless, you feel no shame before others or even before yourselves, for banishing Demosthenes on the same charge on which you acquitted Aristogeiton.[87] [38] You did not grant me what others have because they dare to scorn you and take it from you, namely, the possibility of collecting, if I can, the debts owed to me and raising contributions from my friends,[88] for me to settle my account with you, so that I would not be seen wandering in a foreign land, with old age and exile as my reward for what I did on your behalf, a reproach to all those who wronged me.

[39] I wanted to return home as a result of your gratitude and magnanimity, and to find that the false charges unjustly leveled against me

---

[86] Probably this is *Letter 2* (*Concerning His Own Return*): see the Introduction to this letter.

[87] On Aristogeiton, see 16n.

[88] It was quite normal for someone who had been fined or was in debt to ask his friends for an interest-free loan (*eranos*) in order to settle that debt.

had been removed, and so I asked for immunity only for the period you set for the payment of the fine, but you did not allow this. Instead, I am told, you ask, "Who is stopping him from coming here and doing this?" [40] Gentlemen of Athens, I know how to feel shame, and to understand that my political career on your behalf does not merit my current predicament. I have lost my property because of these men. I was persuaded to underwrite their payments in advance so that they might not have to pay double what they were unable to pay once.[89] If I return home with your goodwill, I might perhaps recover part, if not all, of these loans and might not live badly for the rest of my life. However, if I return as those who talk like this about me demand, then I will be trapped in shame, poverty, and fear all together.

[41] You do not think about any of these things, but begrudging me even a few kind words, you will stand by and see me die, if that should happen, because of you, for there is no one else I can beseech but you. At that point, I am quite certain that you will say that I have been treated terribly, when it will be no good for either you or me. You certainly should not expect that I have property apart from my tangible assets,[90] which I am relinquishing. I would like to collect the remainder if you treat me humanely, not maliciously, and give me the chance to do this safely. [42] For indeed you will never show that I took money from Harpalus;[91] for neither was I convicted of guilt nor did I take any money. But if you look to the famous prestige of the Areopagus Council, remember the trial of Aristogeiton and hide your heads in shame—I have no milder advice for those who wronged me. [43] For surely you cannot say it was right, after information was given

---

[89] A debt was doubled if not paid by the due date under Athenian law (*Ath. Pol.* 48.1, with Rhodes 1981, pp. 559 and 599). Demosthenes evidently lost his property by lending money to others so that they could pay their fines on time. If he was allowed to return, he may have been able to recoup some of his losses.

[90] The Greek word *phaneros* means visible, and here its sense is visible assets such as real estate and household property, as opposed to loans and deposits.

[91] Demosthenes means as a bribe, for according to Hyperides (5.12–13), he apparently admitted he took money as a loan to the Theoric Fund (on which see 3.2n50): see Worthington 1992, pp. 69–73.

in the same words by the same Council, that he was acquitted and I was condemned—you are not so irrational as that! I do not deserve it; it is not right for me; I am no worse than he, though I admit I am unlucky thanks to you. How could I not be unlucky, for, on top of my other troubles, it turns out that I must compare myself to Aristogeiton, and worse still, I am condemned and he got away safely?

[44] Do not think that I am angry when I say this, for I would not feel that way towards you. Those who are wronged get certain relief from telling what they have suffered, just as those in pain do from moaning. And I feel the same goodwill towards you as I would pray you have towards me. I have made this clear in everything I have done—and I will continue to do so. [45] From the outset I realized that every man who enters public life, if he is a just citizen, should have the same attitude to his fellow citizens as children to their parents; he should pray that they should be especially fair to him but should accept them as they are with goodwill. To yield in such circumstances is judged by the wise to be an honorable and creditable victory. Farewell.

LETTER 4. CONCERNING THE SLANDERS OF THERAMENES

Introduction

Alexander is said in *Letter* 1.13 to be dead, and this fourth letter says nothing about the king, which Goldstein (1968) believes makes it predate the first. On the surface, the letter appears to be a reply to the accusation of (the unknown) Theramenes that Demosthenes is cursed and brings only bad luck, and as such, it contains much invective against him (1–2, 4, 11–12). However, buried within it is Demosthenes' claim that Athens is the most fortunate *polis* of all and the one most dear to the gods (3). The claim is supported by reference to oracular pronouncements testifying that Good Fortune now lives in Athens (3–4) and that Demosthenes' policy to Macedonia ultimately proved beneficial to the city (5–9).

Letter 4. Concerning the Slanders of Theramenes

[1] Demosthenes to the Council and the Assembly sends greetings. Among the slanderous things I hear that Theramenes has said about

me, he has accused me of being a jinx.[92] The fact that the man does not know that abuse, which attributes no wickedness to the person against whom it is aimed, is not taken seriously by sensible people does not surprise me. Indeed, it would be more astonishing if a man had any understanding of these things, who lives a life of insolence, who is not a citizen by nature, and who was brought up from childhood in a brothel[93] than if he has no knowledge at all. [2] If I ever return and am pardoned, I shall try to talk to him about his drunken abuse of both you and me, and I think that, although he has no shame, I will make him more reasonable. Meanwhile, to further our common interest, I want to make clear to you in a letter what my thoughts are on this subject. Listen then and pay close attention, for I think they are worth both hearing and remembering.

[3] I consider your city the most fortunate of all cities and most beloved to the gods, and I know that in their oracles Zeus of Dodona and Dione and Pythian Apollo[94] are always saying this, and they confirm with their seal that Good Fortune lives among you in the city.[95] Now, when the gods show something about the future, they are clearly making a prediction; but when their words refer to past events, they mean then to refer to the past. [4] What I have done as a politician among

---

[92] The opening of the letter is abrupt and dramatic; there is no attempt at a *captatio benevolentiae,* but Theramenes is blamed from the outset. Demosthenes is accused of inflicting bad luck on the state in Din. 1.31–33. In the works that survive, Demosthenes is the only Attic orator who uses the Greek word *dustychian* ("bad luck") in the sense of "jinx" (cf. Dem. 18.270, 19.259, 265).

[93] The Greek word here more normally means "workshop" (cf. Demosthenes' criticism of Aeschines in 18.258–262). However, the alternative meaning "brothel" suits the sense better, given Demosthenes' abuse of Theramenes; perhaps it even is meant to suggest that he was a bastard and so not an Athenian citizen.

[94] The oracle of Zeus at Dodona, in Epirus, was the oldest in Greece and the second most important in Greece after that of Pythian Apollo at Delphi. Zeus' consort at Dodona was Dione (= Aphrodite), not his "usual" wife, Hera.

[95] Lycurgus may have introduced the cult of Good Fortune to Athens in the Piraeus (*IG* ii² 1035, 44 and 478), as part of his religious reforms after the Battle of Chaeronea ([Plut.], *Moralia* 852b). Epigraphical evidence attests sacrifices to Good Fortune in 334/3, 33/2, 331/0 (*IG* ii² 1496, 76, 107, and 148).

you belongs to the past, and as a result of this the gods have called you fortunate. Yet, how is it right that those who followed someone's advice are called fortunate, but the person dispensing that advice is called the opposite? We can only conclude that the gods attested the public good fortune when I was an adviser, and they cannot lie, but the personal slander that Theramenes directs against me has been spoken by an insolent, shameless, and ignorant man.

[5] Moreover, you will find that the fortune you enjoy is good not only according to the oracles of the gods but also if you consider the facts themselves and examine them properly. In fact, if you are willing to look at events in human terms, you will discover that our city has become most fortunate thanks to the advice I gave. However, if you try to get things reserved for the gods alone, you reach for the impossible. [6] What is it that is reserved for the gods but impossible for mankind? To have control of all the blessings there are, so that they can have them for themselves and give them to others, and for the rest of time they never suffer or come near suffering anything harmful. Since these principles are firmly established, as is proper, consider your own situation when compared to that of other men. [7] For no one is so foolish as to say that what happened to the Spartans, whom I did not advise,[96] or the Persians,[97] to whom I never went, is preferable to your state of affairs,[98]

---

[96] In 331 the Spartan king Agis III went to war against Antipater and attempted to unite the Greeks under him. There was debate in Athens as to whether the city should support Agis (Diodorus Siculus 17.62.7), but Demosthenes successfully advised against it. This was just as well, for only a few states rallied to Agis, and in early 330 Antipater defeated and killed him at the Battle of Megalopolis (Diodorus Siculus 17.63.1–3; Curtius 6.1). See further Worthington 2000, pp. 90–113, citing bibliography.

[97] Alexander the Great defeated the Persians in three set battles: Granicus in 334, Issus in 333, and Gaugamela in 331. Although Demosthenes did not go to Persia, he did scheme with the Persian King Darius III against Alexander until the time of Issus: see further Worthington 2000. On the three battles, see Bosworth 1988, pp. 40–85, and Worthington 2004a, pp. 73–134.

[98] Although the Macedonians controlled Greece, the Athenians were allowed to keep their fleet, their democracy was not ended, and freedom of speech was still permitted in the city.

to say nothing of the Cappadocians and Syrians⁹⁹ and the people living in the land of India at the far end of the world,¹⁰⁰ all of whom have suffered many terrible and grievous calamities. [**8**] But by Zeus, everyone will agree that you are doing better than these but that you are worse off than the Thessalians and Argives and Arcadians,¹⁰¹ or some others, who were in an alliance with Philip. In fact, however, you are far better off than these, not only because you are not enslaved (what else is as important as that?) but also because, whereas they are all considered responsible for the calamities that have afflicted the Greeks through Philip and their enslavement, and because of this they are rightly hated, [**9**] people see that you fought on behalf of the Greeks with your bodies and property and city and land and everything. In return for this, you deservedly have great renown and eternal gratitude from those who want to do justice. Therefore, thanks to my advice, our city has fared the best of those states that resisted Philip, and it has gained a greater reputation than those that cooperated with him.

[**10**] It is for these reasons that the gods give you favorable oracles and divert the unjust slander onto the head of the slanderer.¹⁰² Anyone

---

⁹⁹ Alexander's general Antigonus fought three battles in Cappadocia before the area was subdued, and Cappadocian losses were heavy at the battles of Granicus and Gaugamela. In Syria, Alexander's sieges of Tyre and of Gaza in 332 ended in the mass slaughter of the men and the selling of all women and children into slavery. On the sieges, see Bosworth 1988, pp. 65–68, and Worthington 2004a, pp. 105–112.

¹⁰⁰ India was considered to be at the end of the world. Alexander fought a spectacular battle against the Indian prince Porus at the Hydaspes River in 326. On the Indian campaign, see Worthington 2004a, pp. 197–232, and esp. Bosworth 1996.

¹⁰¹ Philip was forced to intervene in Thessaly several times in his reign in order to protect his southern border. In 352 he was elected its *tagos* or archon (leader) for life, giving him control of Thessaly as well as some command over its army. Argos and Arcadia, allies of Thebes until the Peace of Philocrates of 346, were instrumental in involving Philip in Peloponnesian affairs in order to combat the power of Sparta. For example, in 344 Argos (and Messene), at war with Sparta, allied with Philip and received mercenary support. Argos was previously mentioned by Isocrates in his *To Philip* of 346 as a state to be courted by the king if he wanted to expand his power in the Peloponnese (5.30, 73–75; cf. 50–55).

¹⁰² That is, Theramenes.

would know this, who chose to examine his way of life. For he voluntarily engages in conduct that someone might wish on him in a curse. [**11**] He is an enemy to his parents,[103] and a friend of Pausanias the prostitute;[104] he bullies like a man but is treated like a woman. He triumphs over his father but is defeated by vices. He delights in things that disgust everyone else, foul language, and recounting matters that pain those listening; but he does not stop talking, as if he were a simple person speaking his mind. [**12**] I would not have written this letter if I did not want to awaken your memory of his evil ways. For the things that someone would be reluctant to speak about and guard against writing about, and I think would disgust a person to hear, each of you is reminded by these words and knows this man's terrible and debauched habits. In this way, I have said nothing indecent, and this man is a reminder of his own depravity to all who see him. Good luck.

LETTER 5. TO HERACLEODORUS

Introduction

This letter purports to have been written to a certain Heracleodorus, when Demosthenes heard from Menecrates that Aratus had summarily arrested his friend Epitimus and that Heracleodorus was supporting the arrest (1). All these people are otherwise unknown, and the authenticity of this letter is highly suspect. For one thing, the events that led to Epitimus' arrest are surprisingly ignored. Furthermore, the reference to the writer as a young man (5) points to a date of 355 or earlier, but all of Demosthenes' letters were written during his exile in 323, when writing letters would have been necessary. As the DeWitts suggest in the Loeb edition (pp. 262–263), Heracleodorus could have been a citizen of a neighboring city, such as Corinth, in which case Demosthenes was appealing on behalf of a friend in another city. However, the letter seems less of an appeal and more of a vehicle to praise Plato's school, with which Demosthenes (to our knowledge) had no formal

---

[103] In Athens, children were legally bound to support their parents in old age and to give them a proper burial: *Ath. Pol.* 56.6 (with Rhodes 1981, *ad loc.*); Dem. 24.103–107 (the law is quoted at 105); cf. Lacey 1968, pp. 116–118.

[104] Otherwise unknown.

connection. Thus, it was probably a later forgery, written to make it appear that the greatest Greek orator had praised Plato.

Letter 5. To Heracleodorus

[1] Demosthenes sends good wishes to Heracleodorus. I do not know whether to believe or disbelieve the news that Menecrates has reported to me. For he said that Epitimus has been informed against and summarily arrested[105] by Aratus and that you undertook the prosecution and were the most harmful of all to him. I entreat you in the name of Zeus, god of friendship, and all the gods, not to put me in a disagreeable and sordid situation. [2] Know well that apart from my concern for Epitimus' safety and my belief that it would be a great misfortune if he were to suffer something and you were partly to blame, I am ashamed to face those who know the reports I have uttered to everyone about you. I was convinced I spoke the truth, not because of my own experience in associating with you [3] but because I saw that as you gained a reputation you had also received an education, and that this was gained from studying with Plato—an education that avoids trying to get the better of people and the sophistries that come with this,[106] but has been shown to do everything for the sake of goodness and justice. By the gods, I think it would be impious for a man who has received this education to lie and not be good to everyone. [4] It would also be most difficult for me if I set out to feel goodwill towards you, and then I was forced to switch to the opposite opinion, as I would if I thought I had been slighted and deceived—and even if I deny it, you must believe that it will be so. [5] If you sneer at us because we have not achieved prominence,[107] beware that you

---

[105] The *endeixis* procedure went in tandem with the *apagōgē* procedure and was a public denunciation of someone. In an *apagōgē*, a person arrested the accused and took him straight to the prison, whereas in an *endeixis* the appropriate magistrates (usually the Eleven) were first approached. These had the accused person arrested until his trial. If found guilty, the punishment was death (Dem. 20.156). On the procedure, see esp. Hansen 1976; cf. MacDowell 1978, pp. 75 and 165–166.

[106] The author subscribes here to Plato's view that the sophists were professional teachers who taught how to use clever arguments so as to succeed in public life.

[107] For the date of this letter, see its Introduction.

too were once young and of the same age as we are now, and you have become who you are by giving advice and taking action. The same thing might also happen to me. For I am a good orator, and with fortune helping out the action may also follow.

[6] Now, a fine contribution would be a just favor in return,[108] which you can do for me. Do not be led or controlled by anyone whose wisdom is less than yours, but persuade those men to your way of thinking. Act in such a way that we are not deprived of any opinion that we agreed upon, but that Epitimus may find safety and deliverance from his troubles. I myself will come when you say is the most opportune time. Send me a letter or even a report as your friend. Good luck.

LETTER 6. TO THE COUNCIL AND THE ASSEMBLY OF THE ATHENIANS

Introduction

The context of this letter is the Lamian War (see the Introduction). It has often been assumed that the letter is spurious, for it lacks the customary opening expected from an exile addressing the Council and People, and no ancient authority cites it. Goldstein (1968) believes it is an Atticist's rhetorical exercise of the second century AD. The common belief is that the battle referred to in the letter is Crannon, at which Antipater defeated the Greeks. Demosthenes had returned to Athens by then, and the letter was obviously written by someone outside the city. However, as I have argued,[109] the battle is most likely Thermopylae, and since the author ends by exhorting the Greeks to take heart, it was probably written during the winter of 323/2, when Antipater was besieged in Lamia and Demosthenes was still in exile.

Letter 6. To the Council and the Assembly of the Athenians

[1] Demosthenes to the Council and the Assembly sends greetings. A letter came from Antiphilus to the allied representatives[110] that

---

[108] This phrase looks like it was a proverbial expression.

[109] Worthington 2003b.

[110] The member states of the Greek alliance that fought Antipater met together as a body (cf. *SIG*³ 327). This meeting was perhaps at Phyle in northern Attica.

satisfied those who wanted to hear good news but left many disagreeable issues for those who support Antipater. These men took the letter from Antipater that came to Dinarchus in Corinth[111] and filled all the cities in the Peloponnese with such stories that the gods should direct their wrath on their heads.[112] [**2**] The man who is arriving now, along with the bearer of my letter, came from Polemaestus to his brother Epinicus.[113] He is loyal to you and is my friend, and when he was brought to me and I heard what he had to say, I decided to send him to you, so that when you clearly heard everything that had taken place in the camp from someone who was present at the battle,[114] you might be encouraged for the present, and for the future might expect that with the favor of the gods the outcome will be what you want. Good luck.

---

[111] This was Dinarchus the Corinthian politician, not the speechwriter, who was also from Corinth but moved to live and work in Athens shortly before Chaeronea in 338: Worthington 1992, pp. 3–5.

[112] When news of Alexander's death reached Athens, Demosthenes, then in exile, went to the Peloponnese personally to win over cities to the Greek resistance to Antipater.

[113] These persons are otherwise unknown; the name Polemaestus is known only from here.

[114] The Battle of Thermopylae, fought soon after the outbreak of the Lamian War in 323, was a Greek victory: see the Introduction.

BIBLIOGRAPHY FOR THIS VOLUME

Adcock, F. E., and D. J. Mosley, 1974: *Diplomacy in Ancient Greece.* London.

Andrewes, A., 1974: *The Greek Tyrants.* London.

Badian, E., 1961: "Harpalus," *JHS* 81: 16–43.

———, 1994: "Agis III: Revisions and Reflections," in *Ventures into Greek History: Essays in Honour of N. G. L. Hammond,* ed. I. Worthington. Oxford: 258–292.

———, 2000: "The Road to Prominence," in *Demosthenes: Statesman and Orator,* ed. I. Worthington. London: 9–44.

Bers, V., 1985: "Dikastic Thorubos," in *Crux: Essays in Greek History Presented to G. E. M. de Ste. Croix on His 75th Birthday,* ed. P. A. Cartledge and F. D. Harvey. London: 1–15.

Blackwell, C. W., 1998: *In the Absence of Alexander: Harpalus and the Failure of Macedonian Authority.* New York.

Blass, F., 1887–1898: *Die attische Beredsamkeit. 2nd ed.* 3 vols. Leipzig.

Bloedow, E. F., 1973: *Alcibiades Reexamined.* Wiesbaden.

Bosworth, A. B., 1988: *Conquest and Empire: The Reign of Alexander the Great.* Cambridge.

———, 1996: *Alexander and the East.* Oxford.

———, 2003: "Why Did Athens Lose the Lamian War?" in *The Macedonians in Athens, 322–229 BC,* ed. O. Palagia and S. V. Tracy. Oxford: 14–22.

Buchanan, J. J., 1962: *Theorika.* New York.

Buckler, J., 2000: "Demosthenes and Aeschines," in *Demosthenes: Statesman and Orator,* ed. I. Worthington. London: 114–158.

Burgess, S., 2005: "The Athenian Eleven: Why Eleven?," *Hermes* 133: 328–336.

Burn, A. R., 1984: *Persia and the Greeks.* London.

Carey, C., 2006: "Epideictic Oratory," in *Blackwell Companion to Greek Rhetoric*, ed. I. Worthington. Oxford.

Cargill, J., 1981: *The Second Athenian League*. Berkeley.

Clavaud, R., 1974: *Démosthène, Discours d'apparat (Épitaphios, Éroticos)*, Budé Text. Paris.

———, 1974: *Démosthène, Prologues*, Budé Text. Paris.

———, 1987: *Démosthène, Lettres et Fragments*, Budé Text. Paris.

Cooper, Craig, 2004: "Demosthenes: Actor on the Political and Forensic Stage," in *Oral Performance and Its Context*, ed. C. M. Mackie. Leiden: 145–161.

Crowther, N. B., 1991: "The Apobates Reconsidered (Demosthenes lxi. 23–9)," *JHS* III: 174–176.

de Brauw, M., 2006: "The Parts of the Speech," in *Blackwell Companion to Greek Rhetoric*, ed. I. Worthington. Oxford.

DeWitt, N. W., and N. J. DeWitt, 1949; repr. 1986: *Demosthenes 7*, Loeb Classical Library. London.

Dobson, J. F., 1919: *The Greek Orators*. London.

Dover, K. J., 1978: *Greek Homosexuality*. New York.

Faraguna, M., 2003: "Alexander and the Greeks," in *Brill's Companion to Alexander the Great*, ed. J. Roisman. Leiden: 99–130.

Forrest, W. G. G., 1966: *The Emergence of Greek Democracy*. London.

Golden, Mark, 1998: *Sport and Society in Ancient Greece*. Cambridge.

Goldstein, J. A., 1968: *The Letters of Demosthenes*. New York.

Green, P., 1996: *The Greco-Persian Wars*. Berkeley.

Grenfell, P., and A. S. Hunt, eds., 1906: *The Hebeh Papyri*, vol. I. London.

Halperin, David, 1990: *One Hundred Years of Homosexuality*. London.

Hammond, N. G. L., and G. T. Griffith, 1979: *A History of Macedonia*, vol. 2. Oxford.

Hammond, N. G. L., and F. W. Walbank, 1988: *A History of Macedonia*, vol. 3. Oxford.

Hansen, M. H., 1976: *Apagoge, Endeixis and Ephegesis against Kakourgoi, Atimoi and Pheugontes*. Odense.

———, 1991: *The Athenian Assembly in the Age of Demosthenes*. Oxford.

Harris, H. A., 1972: *Sport in Greece and Rome*. London.

Harrison, A. R. W., 1968–1971: *The Law of Athens*. 2 vols. Oxford.

Harvey, F. D., 1985: "*Dona Ferentes*: Some Aspects of Bribery in Greek Politics," in *Crux: Essays in Greek History Presented to G. E. M. de Ste.*

Croix on His 75th Birthday, ed. P. A. Cartledge and F. D. Harvey. London: 76–117.

Jordan, B., 1975: *The Athenian Navy in the Classical Period.* Berkeley.

Kagan, D., 1981: *The Peace of Nicias and the Sicilian Expedition.* Ithaca, NY.

———, 1991: *Pericles of Athens and the Birth of Democracy.* New York.

Kennedy, G., 1963: *The Art of Persuasion in Greece.* Princeton.

———, 1994: *A New History of Classical Rhetoric.* Princeton.

Lacey, W. K., 1968: *The Family in Classical Greece.* London.

Loraux, N., 1986: *The Invention of Athens: The Funeral Oration in the Classical City,* trans. A. Sheridan. Cambridge, MA.

MacDowell, D. M., 1978: *The Law in Classical Athens.* London.

Mitchel, F. W., 1970: "Lykourgan Athens: 338–322," in *Semple Lectures,* vol. 2. Cincinnati, OH.

Rahe, P. A., 1981: "The Annihilation of the Sacred Band at Chaeronea," *AJA* 85: 84–87.

Rennie, W., 1931: *Demosthenis Orationes,* vol. 3, Oxford Classical Text. Oxford.

Rhodes, P. J., 1981: *A Commentary on the Aristotelian Athenaion Politeia.* Oxford.

Roebuck, C., 1948: "The Settlement of Philip II with the Greek States in 338 B.C.," *CP* 43: 73–92.

Roisman, J., 2006: "Rhetoric, Manliness and Context," in *Blackwell Companion to Greek Rhetoric,* ed. I. Worthington. Oxford.

Rupprecht, A., 1927: "Die Demosthenische Prooemiensammlung," *Philologus* 82: 365–432.

Ryder, T. T. B., 2000: "Demosthenes and Philip II," in *Demosthenes: Statesman and Orator,* ed. I. Worthington. London: 45–89.

Sealey, B. R. I., 1993: *Demosthenes and His Time: A Study in Defeat.* New York.

Swoboda, R., 1887: *De Demosthenis quae feruntur prooemiis.* Vienna.

Usher, S., 1999: *Greek Oratory: Tradition and Originality.* Oxford.

Wallace, R. W., 1989: *The Areopagos Council.* Baltimore, MD.

Whitehead, D., 2000: *Hypereides: The Forensic Speeches.* Oxford.

Worthington, I., 1992: *A Historical Commentary on Dinarchus: Rhetoric and Conspiracy in Later Fourth-Century Athens.* Ann Arbor, MI.

———, 1994a: "The Harpalus Affair and the Greek Response to the Macedonian Hegemony," in *Ventures into Greek History: Essays in*

Honour of N. G. L. Hammond, ed. I. Worthington. Oxford: 307–330.

————, 1994b: "History and Oratorical Exploitation," in *Persuasion: Greek Rhetoric in Action,* ed. I. Worthington. London: 109–129.

————, 1999: *Greek Orators,* vol. 2, *Dinarchus 1 and Hyperides 5 and 6.* Warminster.

————, 2000: "Demosthenes (In)activity during the Reign of Alexander the Great," in *Demosthenes: Statesman and Orator,* ed. I. Worthington. London: 90–113.

————, 2003a: "Alexander's Destruction of Thebes," in *Crossroads of History: The Age of Alexander the Great,* ed. W. Heckel and L. A. Tritle. Claremont, CA: 65–86.

————, 2003b: "The Authenticity of Demosthenes' Sixth Letter," *Mnemosyne* 56: 585–589.

————, 2003c: "The Authorship of the Demosthenic *Epitaphios,*" *Museum Helveticum* 60: 152–157.

————, 2004a: *Alexander the Great: Man and God,* rev. & enlarged ed. London.

————, 2004b: "Oral Performance in the Athenian Assembly and the Demosthenic *Prooemia,*" in *Oral Performance and Its Context,* ed. C. M. Mackie. Leiden: 129–143.

Worthington, I., C. Cooper, and E. Harris, 2001: *Dinarchus, Lycurgus, and Hyperides,* The Oratory of Classical Greece 5. Austin, TX.

Yunis, H., 1996: *Taming Democracy.* Ithaca, NY.

INDEX